P9-BBV-857

CHARACTER EDUCATION

Grades K–6
Year 1

by John Heidel and
Marion Lyman-Mersereau

Incentive Publications, Inc.
Nashville, Tennessee

Acknowledgments

We would like to acknowledge the many people who supported us in this project. We are indebted to these people who have given of their time and energy to help bring this project to completion.

First, we would like to name the Character Education Committee of Punahou School which conceived of the idea for this project. They set us on the right path with suggestions for what they need, as teachers, to better help in the intentional character education of our students. Special thanks to the Review Committee who offered encouragement and thoughtfully critiqued our work.

In addition, we would like to thank the many other people who provided their time and expertise in developing this complete Character Education program.

Illustrated by Marta Drayton
Cover by Bill Latta
Edited by Jennifer E. Janke

Library of Congress Catalog Card Number: 98-75493
ISBN 0-86530-427-0

PRINTED IN THE UNITED STATES OF AMERICA

TABLE OF CONTENTS

INTRODUCTION

Twenty-five hundred years ago, Socrates defined education as helping students gain both knowledge and virtue, to become both smart and good. In recent decades schools sometimes consciously and sometimes unconsciously have lost their focus on this historic mission. Now, however, educators are being called back to help children gain the virtues, the embedded habits, which constitute good character. Often those calling for character education are parents. Increasingly, they are politicians articulating the will of worried citizens. A few scholars have recognized the current lack in our schools and have become champions for character education. While these voices have been articulate in pointing out the problems of a value-neutral school or a school that rejects responsibility for character formation, these voices are limited. They lack the knowledge of and experience with the instructional issues surrounding this topic. They do not speak to the real world of schools. The authors of this book possess that knowledge and experience.

John Heidel and Marion Lyman-Mersereau have written a book that takes character education to a new level, a level that enables teachers and administrators to go beyond the abstract into that real world of their classrooms and their schools. *Character Education* is based on the authors' action research project at one of the truly lighthouse schools of our nation, the Punahou School in Hawaii.

The book reflects a complete plan for engaging a school community in the mission of character development. Central to their work and to the organization of the book is a school-wide, monthly focus on a particular virtue, such as respect or courage. In this, they are addressing one of the core problems with school's efforts to respond to the call for character education. Americans, and particularly American educators, have frequently replaced the language of moral values and virtue with the language of psychology. Cheating is referred to as "inappropriate behavior" rather than "wrong." The goal has been "student development" and "adjustment," but development *into what* and adjust *to what* has been left vague or unstated. This book and the program it offers educators, while on the one hand being new and fresh, returns us to an older, richer language system, one based on views of human excellence.

Over a two-year cycle, students are introduced to a deeper meaning of common words, such as loyalty, commitment and wisdom. It is here that the authors' gifts as educators become apparent. Students are not simply told the meaning of these virtue words. They are immersed in them. During the months that a particular word is being studied, each day there is a new activity which will give them greater experience and thus deeper understanding of the concept behind the word. Activities range from journal writing to a structured conversation with parents, from creating a poster about the virtue to listing ways students can practice the virtue in their everyday lives.

One of the most plaguing problems of American education is the continuing search for "the one right way": the one right way to teach reading, the one right way to evaluate student performance, the one right way to discipline students. As character education is again becoming a concern of educators, this same one-right-way mentality is becoming evident. The authors of *Character Education* take a very different approach, one that recognizes that children have very different ways of learning and that the best way to master something is to acquire it in several different learning modes. Therefore, the book offers students and teachers a rich reservoir of stories, sayings, and biographical sketches, which together bring out the depth of these concepts and show how they exist in a human life.

Character formation has been described as what we do to help students *know the good, love the good,* and *do the good.* This book addresses all dimensions of that description. The great power and benefit of *Character Education* is its appeal to the student's head, heart, and hands.

Kevin Ryan
Director of the Center for the Advancement of Ethics and Character,
Boston University

PURPOSE

Since one of the primary concerns of this program specifically relates to the total development of students, it is important to remember what a complete student is. A complete student is one which succeeds academically, but also portrays a strong moral character, with a clear sense of right and wrong.

It is probably a good exercise to reflect on how educators are doing. Most people would agree that schools across the country are doing well with academic goals and not so well with character goals. We have many students who don't know how to properly love themselves or each other or who cheat on their schoolwork. There is teasing, gossiping, inappropriate language, and stealing. There are problems with litter and a general lack of common courtesy and good manners. We have a lot of work to do before we can fulfill the dream of a nation filled with complete students.

Thomas Lickona, developmental psychologist and author of *Educating for Character*, asserts that " . . . character must be broadly conceived to encompass the cognitive, affective, and behavioral aspects of morality. Good character consists of knowing the good, loving the good, and doing the good. Schools must help children understand the core values, adopt or commit to them, and then act upon them in their own lives."

While it might be difficult to teach values, the educational process can at least make certain universal values known to our students. Students can be motivated and inspired to incorporate these values into their lives. The final step of acting out these values can be taken as we give our students opportunity for community service and show them how these values can be acted out in the community, on the playground, in the cafeteria, and in the classroom.

The purpose of this program is to design a structure whereby we can be more focused and intentional in our efforts to provide character education. Teachers should keep in touch with each other about activities that work; and design ways to involve parents and the wider community, so the values will be reinforced. Teachers need to be conscious of who they are as role models and what values are reflected by their actions.

In all ways, our purpose is to assist teachers in their efforts to create a classroom environment where students can grow socially and spiritually, as well as intellectually. If these ideas prove useful we will be very gratified. We acknowledge the right of teachers to make this choice and to decide on their level of involvement.We know teachers enjoy autonomy, so there is room for flexibility and the development of personal style.

There has been a lot written about the present moral environment from which our children and youth choose their values. We know about the decline of the family, the lack of good adult models, the pervasive influence of the media, the problems of public schools, and the troubling trends in youth character. Another reason for this changing scene of morality can be traced through the gradual shift in the operative values that have characterized American life. Since the arrival of the Puritans and their lifestyle of honesty, faith, and hard work, there has been a big change. Sociologist Max Lerner made a study of American values in the mid-1950s and published his findings in *America As A Civilization* in 1957. He maintains that the idealistic values of early America became contaminated by money, materialism, competition, and success. "By the turn of the twentieth century a new pattern of life purposes emerged. Its components were success, prestige, money, power, and security." This "five-goal system" seemed to characterize the basic drives and behavioral patterns of most Americans. These five questionable values are alive and well today.

We are hopeful this program will offer other choices and have a positive impact on the daily life within each classroom and with relationships outside the classroom. This is the primary step that educators can take in reordering the moral environment of America with universal values that affirm life and enhance everyone's health and happiness. We can play an important role in the process of restoring a sense of what is right and good for our common life as Americans.

VALUE OF THE MONTH

The framework around which this project is designed is the idea of emphasizing a specific value each month. We chose eighteen values to be the featured values over a two year cycle and 36 others as supportive values. We decided on eighteen because that would give us a two-year cycle of nine values a year. This way we won't be repeating the same values each year and, with a different focus in each grade level, the values should stay fresh.

There is a specific reason for beginning with respect, following with responsibility, and leading toward compassion, faith, and commitment. It will be explained how one leads to the next and how each remains connected to all of the previous values. Some relate to seasonal themes and others become part of a total picture. However, this format is completely flexible and educators may develop their own schedule if students or current events warrant it.

VALUE OF THE MONTH BY TWO-YEAR CYCLE

In the first year students will study:

September	**Respect**	*Acceptance*	*Kindness*
October	**Responsibility**	*Self-discipline*	*Reliability*
November	**Compassion**	*Service*	*Generosity*
December	**Faith**	*Hope*	*Trust*
January	**Commitment**	*Loyalty*	*Effort*
February	**Love**	*Friendship*	*Sincerity*
March	**Wisdom**	*Knowledge*	*Understanding*
April	**Health**	*Holistic Living*	*Serenity*
May	**Humor**	*Joy*	*Enthusiasm*

In the second year, students will expand their character development by learning about:

September	**Honesty**	*Integrity*	*Truth*
October	**Cooperation**	*Family*	*Unity*
November	**Humility**	*Gratitude*	*Appreciation*
December	**Peace**	*Harmony*	*Forgiveness*
January	**Patience**	*Perseverance*	*Confidence*
February	**Courage**	*Tenacity*	*Conviction*
March	**Creativity**	*Wonder*	*Resourcefulness*
April	**Environmental Awareness**	*Beauty*	*Sacrifice*
May	**Freedom**	*Social Justice*	*Equality*

LEVELS OF FACULTY INVOLVEMENT

Basic

Aware of how busy teachers are and how much is already asked, the basic involvement is quite simple. Yet, if we accept this project as important, there is great value in everyone's involvement. It will send a clear message to the students and the wider community of the school's intention. Hopefully, there will be a general feeling of cohesion as teachers share stories about what works and as students talk about each value from their own experience.

Therefore, basic involvement would mean supporting and following the value-of-the-month idea. Specifically, it would mean posting a sign bearing the current month's value, making the students aware of it, finding a connection with your curriculum once a week, and citing an example of someone acting out that value once a week; preferably "catching a student," but also examples from the community and the world. You can take this as far as your time and interest allow; from a short announcement to a discussion.

A Little Extra

You may want to do a little extra for any of the following reasons: the value of the month goes well with your subject area or curriculum, it relates to a current event or issue within the school or worldwide, it reflects one of your concerns, or you just want to explore the possibilities a little more.

In that case, use the extensive information provided on each value in this handbook. There will be suggested activities and, where appropriate, material that will deal with specific issues such as inappropriate language, cheating or stealing. These activities will include stories, quotations, material from world religions, biographies of heroes and heroines, values in other languages, discussion questions and community service ideas. Another suggestion is to follow up a school assembly presentation with a discussion or writing assignment. This level of involvement would mean utilizing these resources two or three times a month.

Beyond the Call

Some people may become so excited about the possibilities of this program that they will use many or all of the suggested calendar of activities. In that case, go for it!

Calendar

At the beginning of each month there is a calendar of suggested activities outlining a lesson plan for that month. No matter the level of involvement chosen, this calendar should help educators fit *Character Education* into their monthly routine. These calendars show daily activities which focus on the value of that month. The calendar can be used to help educators develop creative ways to teach *Character Education.* The schedule need not be followed exactly—this is only one example of how a *Character Education* lesson plan might look

COMMENTS FROM TEACHERS

- I hope we will continue to enlarge/improve this program. Hopefully, teachers of English and perhaps social studies will have students writing on the monthly topics in character education.

- I am so pleased that Punahou has included values as an integral part of our curriculum. As an educator, there is no way I would downplay knowledge; yet as a parent and concerned adult I believe that to be truly enlightened, a person must possess clear and honorable values and a moral character.

- I can't help but feel that our focus on values has brought about a positive change in our day-to-day goings-on. Good mornings and pleases and thank-yous abounded . . .

- The Character Education Handbook filled with guidelines and ideas for the incorporation of given values into the daily curriculum is one of the most significant steps that has taken place at Punahou . . . It resets a standard that speaks to the community at large about Punahou's stand regarding the necessity of spiritual values in daily living.

- I felt the character education program was a great success. Having the quotes in the daily bulletin and the signs in the classroom, cafeteria—everywhere—was very effective; it kept those values in the forefront of our day . . . [it] made us realize that these values were not just something to "teach" our kids, but they were ideals to be sought after by every adult on campus. In a sense they unified us. The chaplains reinforced these values in chapel programs, and the signs/values provided me and my students with a common language for our discussions of themes in our literature.

- The addition and recognition of character education as an integral part of the total curriculum of the school has been long awaited and fully embraced by all students, parents, faculty, staff and administrators alike.

- Start at the kindergarten level and continue through academy years, if not already doing so. There cannot be too much character development!

* These comments were unsolicited and were written after the first year of the program as piloted at the Punahou School.

PARENTAL AND COMMUNITY INVOLVEMENT

The statement, "It takes a whole village to raise a child," refers to the community of support necessary for the upbringing of students. We acknowledge that this is not a task that we educators do alone. Much of a school's success is a result of parental involvement. Parental support in reinforcing a school's educational goals for their children is imperative. We, therefore, feel it is important for parents to be aware of this particular program, so that they may more actively participate in reinforcing these goals of *Character Education.*

Through announcements, newsletters, and various other methods of communication, educators can keep parents informed of the value of the month, related activities, and opportunities to attend workshops or selected speaker engagements.

Our dreams for Character Education go beyond the triangle of parents, teachers, and students to include the community outside of school. As Thomas Lickona writes, the long term success of any character education depends on " . . . the extent to which families and communities join schools in a common effort to meet the needs of children and foster their healthy development."

Here are some excerpts from letters of support our project has received from parents and the community around Punahou School:

I am writing to applaud and commend you for attacking what I think is at the very heart of a world wide epidemic . . . During the next 1½ years, I will encourage physicians to focus on the importance of personal responsibility and other attributes of character building. I will encourage physicians to assist in spreading this message via the media and to address the community with appropriate speeches.

– Carl W. Lehman, M. D.
President, Hawaii Medical Association

While I do teach at a Buddhist-affiliated school, the general philosophy and the values on which the Character Education program is based are universal. I will be sharing the program with all Middle School teachers and the Reverends who instruct the students in religious education.

– Lynette Araki
Hongwanji Mission School

The Character Education program . . . is a breath of fresh air, and I encourage you . . . to vigorously continue this initiative for the sake of our children, our community, and our country.

– M. G. MacLaren

Your "village" concept has led me to conclude that we probably have more villages than we realize . . . , and, more importantly, that those villages don't communicate with each other very well. That is probably our ultimate challenge before we can really solve some of the underlying issues.

– Ed Case
Representative, 23rd District, Hawaii

SUGGESTED LETTER TO PARENTS

Dear K–6 Parents,

This year we will be embarking on a new project in our school, a program on *Character Education.* We would like to keep you informed of our efforts in this area, since we know that "It takes a whole village to raise a child." We, as educators, are only a supplementary part of the ongoing character education in which you are involved with your child.

The values we will be teaching are among those that are universally accepted in a democratic society. As you can see from the list below, there are partner values which accompany the main value of the month. Respect and responsibility are the values for September and October. Respect and responsibility are so inclusive it is understandable why they will be taught first. They are a great foundation on which we can continue to build.

At the beginning of each month, the value being emphasized will be highlighted. We will also have a sign depicting the value of the month, partner values, and a concise definition of the main value for each classroom.

We welcome any input that you may have on our program. We are especially interested in how we can create community awareness and involvement. Thomas Lickona, author of *Educating for Character*, points out that the long term success of any values education depends on " . . . the extent to which families and communities join schools in a common effort to meet the needs of children and foster their healthy development." The values to be taught this year are:

September .... **Respect,** Acceptance, Kindness

October .... **Responsibility,** Self-discipline, Reliability

November .... **Compassion,** Service, Generosity

December .... **Faith,** Hope, Trust

January .... **Commitment,** Loyalty, Effort

February .... **Love,** Friendship, Sincerity

March .... **Wisdom,** Knowledge, Insight

April .... **Health,** Holistic Living, Serenity

May .... **Humor,** Joy, Enthusiasm

We look forward to having you join us in this worthwhile effort to continue to foster the character education which you have already begun with your children.

Sincerely,

September

SUPPORTIVE VALUES **Acceptance • Kindness**

DEFINITIONS **Treating everyone including yourself with dignity.**

"**Respect** means showing regard for the worth of someone or something. It includes respect for self, respect for the rights and dignity of all persons, and respect for the environment that sustains all life. Respect is the restraining side of morality; it keeps us from hurting what we ought to value." (Thomas Lickona) Mutual respect is the way we create a harmonious life with each other; respect is freely given to others and must be earned for oneself.

Acceptance is the approval of a person's worth and agreement with others' individual rights. Tolerance is often listed as an important value, but we have not included it because of the negative connotation of "putting up with someone." Acceptance goes much further. We acknowledge a person's right to disagree with us and we accept their opinion as valid.

Kindness is an expression of love and respect. Kindness puts our feelings of respect into action through words of acceptance, encouragement and support, and through acts of comfort, help and generosity.

PURPOSE Most of the universal values and virtues that contribute to the good of the individual and society and affirm our human dignity are derived from the value of respect (and next month's value of responsibility). If we can provide our students with an understanding of these core qualities, the other values will be more quickly and easily understood. Our purpose this month is to make respect operative in the lives of our students.

Respect — September

Day One: Discuss the meaning of the word respect.	Day Two: With a partner, read and pronounce as best you can the word respect in other languages (see page 19) Research the cultures represented to find out ways self-respect is demonstrated in each.	Day Three: Illustrate an incident in a story (pages 21-24) that demonstrates respect for a person, place or thing.	Day Four: Select a proverb or maxim (page 25) that encourages self-respect. Color it and cut it out to use as a book mark in your social studies text.	Day Five: Read one of the stories about respect from pages 21-24. Discuss, as a class, the message within the story.
Day Six: Discuss with a partner the meaning of self-respect.	**Day Seven:** Name: 1) a family member who demonstrates respect for good health 2) a neighbor who demonstrates respect for children 3) a community member who demonstrates respect for community property	**Day Eight:** Write a letter to tell of your respect for school helpers who work hard to make your school a pleasant place in which to learn and grow.	**Day Nine:** Design and present a "Good Example Award" to a classmate who exemplifies respect for academic excellence in a manner that sets a good example for others.	**Day Ten:** Select a hero or heroine to read about. (See pages 27-28) Draw a picture of this person as you imagine them.
Day Eleven: Design a survey to determine the level of respect shown for your school's environment by its inhabitants.	**Day Twelve:** Create a poster to encourage students to show respect for the school environment. Hang it up outside your classroom door.	**Day Thirteen:** List and analyze ways students in your school demonstrate respect for their teacher.	**Day Fourteen:** List and analyze ways teachers and administrators in your school demonstrate respect for the students.	**Day Fifteen:** In small groups, compare lists made during the past two days—compare and contrast how the lists overlap.
Day Sixteen: Make a list of ways young people can show respect for the elderly in your community.	**Day Seventeen:** Consider ways family members can show respect for each other. Think of one specific thing you can do to increase respect in your family.	**Day Eighteen:** Select the service project (page 30) for demonstrating respect that you feel you could most successfully implement—make a plan for it.	**Day Nineteen:** Create a banner to encourage awareness of and respect for individual differences and cultural diversity in your community. Hang up the banner in a public place such as the library or post office.	**Day Twenty:** Reflect on the meaning of embracing respect for self and others as a life-shaping value.

RESPECT IN OTHER LANGUAGES

Chinese	*zun* *jing*	to honor; to venerate to revere; to respect; to honor; reverent attention to
French	*le respect*	state of mind which makes us treat someone or something with great esteem or consideration, e.g. respect for one's parents or respect for laws.
German	*respekt*	respect, honor
Hawaiian	*ho'ihi*	treated with reverence or respect 'ihi means "sacred, holy, majestic, dignified"
Japanese	*sonkei*	to show respect by offering a glass of wine with a deep bow son -"to offer a glass of wine, or something precious or valuable" kei – "to bow by bending the body, to respect, to be discreet"
Korean	*jon kyong*	look up to with honor; venerate
Latin	*reverentia*	from Latin "respectus" (looking back, consideration, regard: from "re" (back, again) + "spicere" (to look) (something worth looking at again)
Spanish	*respeto*	respect, deference, esteem
Tagalog	*paggalang*	feel or show honor toward others; including their ideas and property

DISCUSSION QUESTIONS

- Do you take care of your friends' toys as carefully as you take care of your own? Why is this important?
- What kinds of daily actions or words show how you respect yourself and others? (being polite, saying thank you, using kind words)
- When you feel sad or angry at the way you've been treated, what can you learn about how you should treat others? (The Golden Rule)
- How do you show respect for the earth? (not destroying flowers or trees, conserving water, not littering)
- When someone is being teased, do you stand up for them and ask the teaser to stop? Why is this important?
- How does the kind of language we use show how much we respect or like ourselves? How do the words we use describe who we are?
- What is gossip?
- What should you do when you hear some gossip about somebody?
- Why is it important to be courteous to each other? Are you courteous to teachers, store clerks, people you meet, everyone?
- Why are table manners important? What are good table manners?
- What have you done in the last two days that indicates your respect for the earth?
- What are some examples of self-respect?
- Why are cleanliness, exercise, healthy eating, language, and everyday manners considered signs of self-respect?

STORIES AND THOUGHTS FROM SPIRITUAL TRADITIONS

Buddhism

Once upon a time in ancient India, there was a very rich man. One day this man decided to invite the Buddha and many monks for lunch. He decorated his home in grand style and arranged for many fine dishes to be served. When the day for the luncheon came, he welcomed the Buddha and the monks with great pomp and ceremony.

Outside the wall of the rich man's house, a very poor man sat by the side of the road outside the gate. Being so poor, he had nothing at all to offer the Buddha. But when he saw the beautiful arrangements the rich man had made, he felt very happy and rejoiced in the rich man's good deeds.

When the luncheon was over, the rich man felt very proud about the grandness of the occasion. Puffed up with pride and expecting to be praised, he asked the Buddha, "Who accumulated the most merit today?" Without hesitation, the Buddha replied, "The old man outside the gate."

When he heard this, the rich man was astonished and very upset. He said, "How can it be? When I have spent so much to offer such a wonderful lunch, how can this penniless pauper have accumulated more merit?" And the Buddha replied, "It is true that you have prepared a fine lunch, but you were motivated by pride and expected recognition from your good deed. With a pure heart and without thought of reward, he has accumulated a huge store of merit."

Respect for others means appreciating their good qualities and rejoicing in their good deeds. Rejoicing in the good deeds of others cuts through all jealousy and resentment.

Hinduism

One is never at fault for obeying one's parents and teachers, for they are God's representatives on this earth.

– Tradition

The first teacher is mother, then father, the school instructors, and finally one's spiritual guide. All of these must be given respect, for they all give us knowledge of this world and the next.

– Tradition

Chinese

"A young man's duty is to behave well to his parents at home and to his elders abroad, to be cautious in giving promises and punctual in keeping them, to have kindly feelings towards everyone, but seeks the intimacy of the Good."

– Confucius

Christianity

A Woman Washes Jesus's Feet

One of the Pharisees, Simon, asked Jesus to come to his home for lunch and Jesus accepted the invitation. As they sat down to eat, a prostitute heard he was there and brought an exquisite flask filled with expensive perfume. Going in, she knelt behind Jesus at his feet, weeping, with her tears falling down upon his feet; and she wiped them off with her hair and kissed them and poured the perfume on them.

When Simon saw what was happening and who the woman was, he said to himself, "This proves that Jesus is no prophet, for if God had really sent him, he would know what kind of woman this one is!"

Then Jesus spoke up and answered his thoughts. "Simon," he said, "I have something to say to you."

"All right, Teacher," Simon replied, "go ahead."

Then Jesus told him this story: "A man loaned money to two people—$5,000 to one and $500 to the other. But neither of them could pay him back, so he kindly forgave them both, letting them keep the money! Which do you suppose loved him most after that?"

"I suppose the one who had owed him the most," Simon answered.

"Correct," Jesus agreed.

Then he turned to the woman and said to Simon, "Look! See this woman kneeling here! When I entered your home, you didn't bother to offer me water to wash the dust from my feet, but she has washed them with her tears and wiped them with her hair. You refused me the customary kiss of greeting, but she has kissed my feet again and again from the time I first came in. You neglected the usual courtesy of olive oil to anoint my head, but she has covered my feet with rare perfume. Therefore, her sins—and they are many—are forgiven, for she loved me much; but one who is forgiven little, shows little love."

And Jesus said to her, "Your sins are forgiven."

Then the men at the table said to themselves, "Who does this man think he is, going around forgiving sins?"

And Jesus said to the woman, "Your faith has saved you; go in peace."

– Bible, Luke 7:36-50

Judaism

The Rabbi's Gift

There was a monastery which had fallen on hard times. At one time its buildings had been filled with young monks, and its big church had resounded with the singing of the chant. Only a handful of old monks were left in the decaying mother house, the abbot and four others. Clearly this was a dying order.

In the deep woods surrounding the monastery there was a little hut which a rabbi had built, and to which, from time to time, he would go to fast and to pray. The monks had become a bit psychic from their years of quiet contemplation and prayer, and they could sense when the rabbi was at his hermitage. They would whisper among themselves, "The rabbi walks in the woods.

Agonizing over the imminent death of his order, the abbot decided to visit the rabbi at his hut, hoping that he might offer some advice that could save the monastery. The rabbi welcomed the abbot at his hut with open arms. The abbot explained the purpose of his visit, and the rabbi empathized with him, replying that it was the same in his town—the spirit seemed to have left the people, and almost no one went to the synagogue anymore. The old rabbi and the old abbot wept together, then they read the Torah together and spoke of deep and profound things. "It has been a wonderful thing that we could meet after all these years," said the abbot, "but please, can you give me some advice that might help save my dying order?"

"I am sorry," replied the rabbi, "I have no advice for you. All I can tell you is that the Messiah is one of you."

The abbot returned to the monastery where the monks questioned him, asking what advice the rabbi had given him. The abbot told them what the rabbi had said, that the Messiah was one of them.

In the months that followed, the monks pondered this idea and wondered what the significance of the rabbi's words could be. "The Messiah is one of us? Could he possibly mean one of us monks right here in this monastery? Well then, which one of us? He probably meant the Father Abbot. Yes, he has been our leader for so long. But then again he might have meant Brother Thomas. He is truly a holy man, a man of light. He couldn't have meant Brother Phillip. Brother Phillip is so crotchety at times and is a thorn in people's sides. Yet when you think about it, Phillip always seem to do and say the right thing at the right time. What about Brother Daniel? No, Brother Daniel is so passive, a real nobody. But then he has a gift for somehow always being there when you need him. Maybe Daniel is the Messiah. Of course the rabbi couldn't mean me. He couldn't possibly mean me. I'm just an ordinary person. Yet what if he did? Could I mean that much to God?"

As they thought about each other in this way, they began to treat each other with a very special reverence on the off chance that one of them might be the Messiah. There was a gentle, wholehearted, human quality about them which was hard to describe but easy to notice.

Visitors to the beautiful forest near the monastery would often picnic on their lawn and wander along its paths. They were deeply moved by the life of these monks. Before long people were coming from far and wide to be nourished by the atmosphere of the place, which was strangely attractive, even compelling, and once again young men were asking to become part of the community. Within a few years, the monastery had become a thriving order, and although the rabbi no longer walked in the woods, thanks to his gift, it was a vibrant center of light and spirituality in the realm.

PROVERBS AND MAXIMS

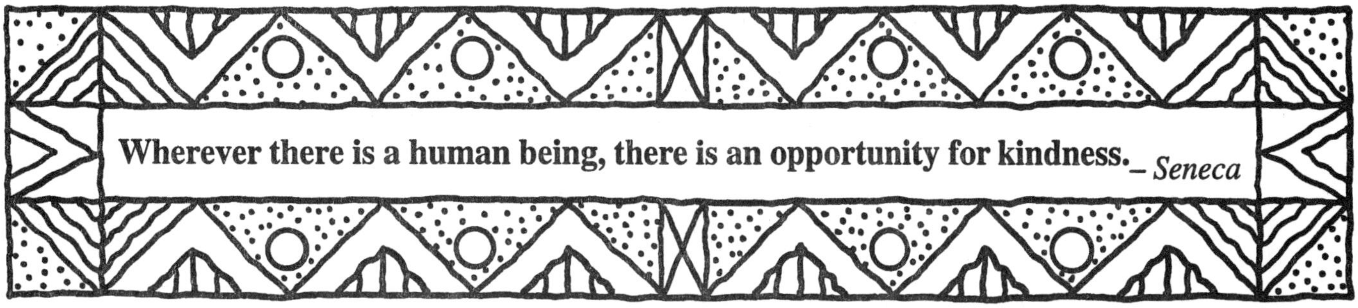

Wherever there is a human being, there is an opportunity for kindness. – *Seneca*

My religion is simple.
My religion is kindness.
– *The Dalai Lama*

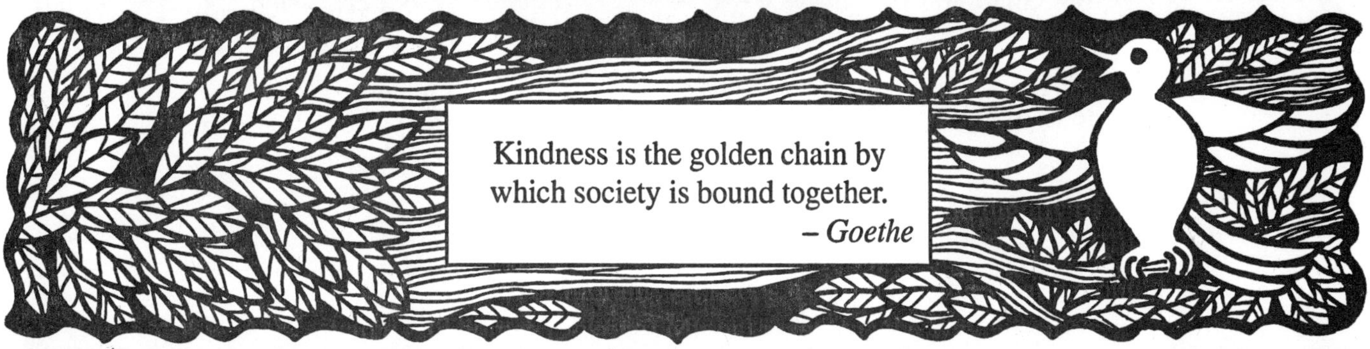

Kindness is the golden chain by which society is bound together.
– *Goethe*

It is the weak who are cruel. Gentleness and kindness can only be expected from the strong.
– *Leo Rosten*

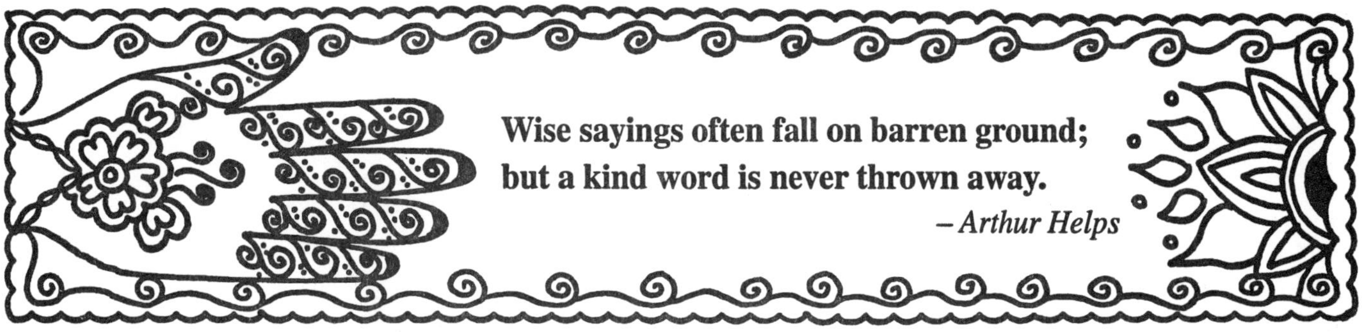

Wise sayings often fall on barren ground; but a kind word is never thrown away.
– *Arthur Helps*

THE GOLDEN RULE THROUGH THE AGES

Zoroastrianism

That nature alone is good which refrains from doing unto another whatsoever is not good for itself. *– Zoroaster, 6th century B.C.E. Dadistan-i-dimik, 94,5*

Buddhism

Hurt not others with that which pains thyself. *– Buddha, 6th century B.C.E. Udana Varga, 5,18*

Taoism

Regard your neighbor's gain as your own gain, and your neighbor's loss as your own loss. *– Tai Shang Kan Ying P'ien*

Confucianism

Is there one maxim which ought to be acted upon throughout one's life? Surely it is the maxim of loving-kindness: Do not do unto others what you do not want others to do unto you. *– Confucius, 6th century B.C.E. The Analects 15, 23*

Greek Philosophy

May I do unto others as I would that they should do unto me. *– Plato, 5th century B.C.E.*

Hinduism

This is the sum of duty: Do naught unto others which would cause you pain if done to you. *– from the Mahabarata, 3rd century B.C.E.*

Judaism

What is hateful to you, do not to your fellowman. That is the entire law; all the rest is commentary. *– Talmud, Shabbat 3id.*

Do not do unto others what thou wouldst not they should do unto thee. *– Rabbi Hillel, 1st century B.C.E.*

Christianity

Do unto others as you would have others do unto you. *– Jesus, 1st century C.E.*

Islam

None of you is a believer until he desires for his brother that which he desires for himself. *– Muhammed, 6th century C.E. Sunnah*

Baha'i

Lay not on any soul a load which ye would not wish to be laid upon you and desire not for anyone the things you would not desire for yourself. *– Baha'ulla, 19th century C.E.*

HEROES AND HEROINES

ABRAHAM LINCOLN (1809–1865)

Born in a log cabin on a farm in Hardin County, Kentucky, Lincoln grew tall and strong from his work on the frontier. He also grew strong in character and was first noticed by the public when he was placed in charge of a small mill and store. He became skilled as a wrestler, debater, military leader and politician. As the sixteenth president of the United States and president during the Civil War, Lincoln was immortalized by his Emancipation Proclamation, his Gettysburg Address, and two outstanding inaugural addresses. He had never learned to hate, and throughout his presidency was committed to restoring the union and freeing the slaves. He respected his enemies and modeled understanding, forgiveness, and kindness.

GOLDA MEIR (1898–1978)

Born in Kiev, Ukraine, she emigrated with her family to Milwaukee, Wisconsin in 1906. She attended a local teachers' college and taught in the public schools until 1921, at which time she left for Palestine and joined Kibbutz Merchavia. She became active in the World Zionist Organization in 1929 and participated in several Jewish agencies and councils. She served as Israel's foreign minister from 1956-1966 and prime minister from 1969-1974. She was a pioneer in struggles leading to the creation of a Jewish state and is described as one of the great women in Jewish history. She was instrumental in securing general peace agreements with Arab nations in the early 1970s.

SHINRAN (1173–1262)

Born in Kyoto, he was a member of the illustrious Fujiwara family, which ruled Japan during the Heian period. He was orphaned at an early age and entered a monastery near Kyoto, where he began an intense study of Tendai Buddhism. He found this unsatisfying and became a disciple of Honen, founder of Jodo, or The Pure Land School. Shinran developed the beliefs of Jodo to its simplest form in order to reach all levels of people. Other established branches of Buddhism regarded his stance as subversive because of its emphasis on the common person, its egalitarian viewpoint, and its simple, individualistic approach to deliverance. Though Shinran was not well-known during his own day, his teachings were known as Jodo Shinoku and became one of the largest Buddhist denominations as well as the major tradition of those Japanese who immigrated to America during the end of the 19th century.

ROGER WILLIAMS (ca. 1603–1683)

Born in London, educated at Cambridge, chaplain to Sir William Masharn of Essex in 1629, Williams became disenchanted with the Anglican Church and sailed for Massachusetts with his wife in 1630. He was banished from Massachusetts in 1635 because he taught that churches in the colonies had not "separated" themselves from the corrupt Anglican Church. In spite of these conservative views, he believed that all men have the same natural rights and should share land equally; he assisted in setting up a democratic land association. He was a champion of the rights of Native Americans and supported the separation of Church and State. He also supported, while disagreeing with, the beliefs of other religious groups such as Quakers and Jews.

PUT RESPECT INTO ACTION

- Practice the Golden Rule.
- Practice Random Acts of Kindness.
- Practice saying “please” and “thank you.”
- Make a point of not teasing and encourage your friends not to.
- Be patient with yourself and others when a mistake is made.
- Discuss with your parents what good manners are.
- Practice your table manners.
- Make an effort to not gossip.
- Make an effort to not swear.
- Be courteous toward everyone.
- Learn how to properly introduce yourself to an adult.
- Practice giving a firm handshake with a friend.
- Remember to raise your hand when you want to speak in class.

COMMUNITY SERVICE IDEAS

- Entertain senior citizens at a retirement home; taking them flowers or small gifts, and singing and talking with them.
- Correspond with students from another country and learn about each other's culture.
- Write thank you letters to community leaders.
- Volunteer with a library for the blind or physically handicapped.
- Volunteer to help with clean-up or gardening chores at a park or other public recreational area.
- Select another school in your community and share with them the meaning of respect. Exchange art projects, school calendars. original writings and note and discuss similarities and differences. Try to exchange visits.
- Survey your school to investigate facilities for handicapped students and visitors. Make recommendations for improvements and conduct a fund-raiser to support those changes.
- Honor Labor Day by showing respect for the working people in your community. Select an important occupation to the community and send them a thank you letter. (i.e. Utility workers, Sanitation workers, Elected Officials, Teachers or Postal Workers)
- Broadcast the message of respect to your community by making posters to display in community centers such as your local post office or grocery store.

BOOKS ON RESPECT

An Angel for Solomon Singer. Cynthia Rylant. New York: Orchard Books, 1992.

The Big Orange Splot. Daniel Manus Pinkwater. New York: Hastings House, 1977.

Fish is Fish. Leo Lionni. New York: Pantheon Books, 1970.

From the Mixed-up Files of Mrs. Basil E. Frankweiler. Elaine Konigsburg. New York: Atheneum, 1967.

Gentle Hands. M.E. Kerr. New York: H & Row, 1978.

The Hundred Penny Box. Sharon Bell Mathis. New York: Viking Press, 1975.

The Rare One. Pamela Rogers. Nashville: Thomas Nelson, Inc., 1974.

Rosie the Cool Cat. Pitor Wilkon. New York: Viking, 1991.

Sea Glass. Laurence Yep. New York: Harper & Row, 1979.

The Story of Abraham Lincoln. Ann Donegan Spencer. La Jolla: Value Communications, Inc., 1977.

The Story of Elizabeth Fry. Spencer Johnson. La Jolla: Value Communications, Inc., 1976.

Throwing Shadows. Elaine Konigsburg. New York: Atheneum, 1979.

Watch Out for the Feet in Your Chicken Soup. Tomie dePaola. Englewood Cliffs: Prentice-Hall, 1974.

The Book of Virtues. William J. Bennett, ed. New York: Simon and Schuster, 1993.

"The Cap that Mother Made" – p. 668

A Call to Character. Colin Greer and Herbert Kohl, eds. New York: Harper Collins Publishers, 1995.

"Among the Tribes" – p. 308

"The Diary of Ann Frank" – p. 292

"The Lion and the Boar" – p. 269

"The Lion, the Witch, and the Wardrobe" – p. 260

"The Scotty Who Knew Too Much" – p. 269

A 5th Portion of Chicken Soup for the Soul. Jack Canfield and Mark Victor Hansen. Deerfield Beach: Health Communications, 1997.

"The Golden Rule" – p. 355

The Moral Compass. William J. Bennett, ed. New York: Simon and Schuster, 1995.

"The Legend of Saint Christopher" – p. 710

Responsibility

SUPPORTIVE VALUES

Self-discipline • Reliability

DEFINITIONS

Taking care of your duties and answering for your actions.

Responsibility means being accountable or answerable to something within one's power. Thomas Lickona calls this the active side of morality. "It includes taking care of self and others, fulfilling our obligations, contributing to our communities, alleviating suffering, and building a better world." (Lickona)

Self-discipline is the disciplined training of one's self with some form of self-improvement in mind. This is a trait used by athletes, artists and musicians and should be used by students in the same way. There is also an important underlying theme of self-control. For personal happiness and social harmony we need to act and speak appropriately.

Reliability means that we can be counted on to follow through on all our responsibilities; our word is trustworthy, we are dependable in achievement, accurate in our assessments and honest in all our dealings.

PURPOSE

Along with respect, responsibility is a core value under which fall several other themes. Lickona's broad definition is connected with other values we will consider later. The emphasis for this month will center on accountability and dependability. Since so many other values relate to respect and responsibility, success in making them understood depends on how well these first two are learned. The goal is to make respect and responsibility central character traits within the lives of all students.

Responsibility — October

Day One: Discuss the meaning of the word responsibility.	**Day Two:** Give examples of how boys and girls in your school demonstrate responsibility for their own health and well-being.	**Day Three:** Whose responsibility is it to see that 1) Your homework is done 2) Your supplies are organized for the day 3) The school building is clean 4) The playground is safe	**Day Four:** Make a poster to encourage people of your age to accept responsibility for conserving earth's natural resources.	**Day Five:** Send a "thank you" message to someone in your community who carries out a responsibility that makes the community a nicer place to live.
Day Six: Name and describe the ways members of the military forces assume special responsibility for citizens of the country they serve.	**Day Seven:** Prepare a journal entry about family members' responsibilities to each other.	**Day Eight:** Suggest to your teacher improvements that could be made in the way irresponsible student behavior is dealt with in your school.	**Day Nine:** Rate yourself _ good _fair _ poor on responsibility for 1) Your own rights and possessions 2) The rights and possessions of others 3) Your own health and safety 4) The health and safety of others. Ponder your answers!	**Day Ten:** Find a news story about a leader who behaved in an irresponsible manner that resulted in pain for the people he or she is responsible for.
Day Eleven: Tell how yesterday's story would have been different had the leader behaved in a responsible manner.	**Day Twelve:** Select a hero from the past or present whose behavior exemplifies a special sense of responsibility for other people. Retell the story to someone else.	**Day Thirteen:** Read *Horton Hatches the Egg* by Dr. Seuss (see page 47 for list of books).	**Day Fourteen:** Design an award for a member of your class that you have observed demonstrating responsibility for the good of the entire class.	**Day Fifteen:** Think of a time when you were held responsible for someone else's behavior. Write or tell about the outcome and how you felt.
Day Sixteen: Write a creative story based on one of the following 1) The life guard whose heroic actions saved a drowning person 2) The lady who rescued a bird with a broken wing 3) A passing teenager who snatched a toddler from the path of a speeding car.	**Day Seventeen:** Ask three people you respect to define responsibility in their own words. Compare the meanings they give your with your own definition. What are the main differences?	**Day Eighteen:** Create a poster or banner to promote awareness of the importance of school spirit and individual responsibility for team efforts.	**Day Nineteen:** Compose a set of guidelines for developing student and teacher responsibility for a creative and challenging classroom climate.	**Day Twenty:** Reflect on what embracing responsibility as a life long value means to you personally.

RESPONSIBILITY IN OTHER LANGUAGES

Chinese	*zé*	duty; responsibility; to lay charge upon; to upbraid; to ask from; to demand
	ren	an official position; an office; to employ; to put in office
French	*la responsibilité*	the ability to make a decision without the need to have the approval of a higher authority; the obligation one has to make up for a mistake, fulfill a duty or a commitment
German	*verantwortung*	to answer for, to account for, to defend, to vindicate; accept the reasons for being accountable
Hawaiian	*kuleana*	right, privilege, concern, responsibility
Japanese	*sekinin*	to condemn someone to carry a heavy task on that person's back seki – to press a person for payment, to condemn, to blame nin – to carry a heavy thing on one's back
Korean	*chaek im*	accountable for given task
Latin	*cura*	from Latin "re" (back) + "spondere" (to pledge)
Spanish	*responsubitidad*	responsibility, liability, accountability
Tagalog	*katungkulan*	take care of one's tasks, duties, debts, and, especially, children

DISCUSSION QUESTIONS

- Is it important for your parents to be able to count on your dependability? When they ask you to clean your room? To follow their directions about personal safety?

- Can you use self-control when you get angry and feel like swearing? Why is this important?

- Can people count on you to always do your best, to speak the truth, and be a good friend?

- Why is "bad language" considered irresponsible behavior?

- Why do people swear?

- What are appropriate exclamations for anger or pain or surprise?

- What are situations when self-control is difficult?

STORIES AND THOUGHTS FROM SPIRITUAL TRADITIONS

Hawaii

The Oyster of Pu'uloa

A long time ago, a great lizard brought a special kind of oyster to Hawaii from far away Tahiti and planted them in Pu'uloa, what is now known as Pearl Harbor. In the kapu protected harbor they grew and multiplied. Kapu meant that there were only certain times of the year that you could gather these oysters from this area. In this way they could grow and provide food for many people.

One day, a woman was gathering seaweed in her basket. As she wandered, pulling little bits of seaweed here and there, she put her hand into a hole and felt an oyster. She looked around to see if anyone was near since she knew that the oysters were kapu or forbidden at this time of year. She took the oyster and hid it under the seaweed in her basket and continued looking for oysters which she loved to eat. When the woman was finished with her gathering, the overseer of the area came to check her basket. She told him that she only had seaweed. He took her basket to see for himself and discovered the oysters. "You have broken the kapu!" he yelled angrily. "You shall be punished." And he took her basket and threw all that she had gathered back into the ocean and then pulled her basket apart. "Now you must leave without anything."

The woman knew she was wrong and that she deserved punishment. She was ashamed of what she had done and walked home feeling very unhappy. The overseer followed her and soon confronted her. "You must give me money," he commanded. "You broke the kapu and this is part of your punishment."

The poor woman felt she had been punished enough and refused the man, but he insisted that she pay. She finally gave him all the money she had, which was only a single coin. The great lizard was very angry at all that she had seen, for she did not believe the woman deserved to be punished twice. In her anger, she took all of the pearls oysters, which she had brought to the harbor, and planted them back in Tahiti, which is now famous for pearls. Because of the irresponsible woman and the overseer, there are no longer any pearls in Pearl Harbor.

India

A Companion in Joy and Sorrow

A hunter discharged his poisoned arrow at a deer. Missing its mark, the arrow pierced a big tree. The poison affected the whole tree; its leaves dropped and it began to dry up. There had lived a parrot a long time in a hollow of the tree. It had become very attached to the tree and so it did not leave the tree. It gave up coming outside the hollow and, for want of anything to eat and drink, was itself reduced to a skeleton. The pious parrot made up its mind to die along with its companion, the tree. Its generosity, fortitude, even-mindedness in pleasure and pain, and spirit of self-sacrifice produced a great change in the atmosphere. Indra's attention was drawn towards it, and he appeared before the bird. The parrot recognized Indra. Thereupon Indra said, "Dear parrot, this tree has neither leaves nor fruits. No bird roosts on it now. There is a vast forest beside you, which contains thousands of beautiful trees laden with fruits and flowers, as also innumerable habitable hollows covered with leaves. This tree is now about to die; it can no longer bear fruits and flowers. Considering all this, why should you not move to some other green tree, leaving this withered one?"

The pious parrot replied in words expressive of commiseration for the tree, "O king of gods, I was born and brought up on this tree; I also learnt some good things here, and it always looked after me as a child. It gave me sweet fruits to eat and also protected me from the attacks of my enemies. Now where should I go for my pleasure, leaving it in such a pitiful plight? Having enjoyed pleasure with it, I shall endure sufferings too with it. It is a matter of great delight to me. Being the lord of the gods, why are you giving me this wrong advice? When it was strong and prosperous, I supported my life under its shelter and now when it is powerless and ruined, how is it possible that I should go away leaving it to its fate?"

Indra was very pleased to hear these sweet and attractive words full of affection from the parrot. He was moved with pity and said, "Parrot, ask any boon of me." The parrot replied, "As you are disposed to confer a boon on me, please grant that this tree, so dear to me, turns as fresh and green as before." Indra watered the tree with a shower of nectar. The tree again bore new branches, leaves and fruits. It attained its full bloom as before and the parrot ascended to heaven when it died as a reward for this ideal behavior.

Pueblo Indian

The Story of Crow and Hawk

Once there was a beautiful black crow. She had a nest on the side of a rocky hillside. She was quite proud of it as it was full of eggs. There she sat waiting for her eggs to hatch. She sat and sat, but nothing happened. She sat some more and still, nothing happened. Finally, Crow got tired of all that sitting, and she just flew away.

The eggs sat in the nest unguarded. They sat and sat, but Crow did not return. After a while, a lovely Hawk flew by. She swooped once over the nest, spotting the eggs. Again she swooped over the nest trying to spot the mother bird. The third time she swooped over the nest she said to herself, "The mother of these eggs no longer cares for them. Poor little eggs. I shall sit on them until the mother returns."

Hawk sat on the eggs. She sat and sat, but nobody came. For days she sat, guarding and warming Crow's eggs. Then one day, the eggs began to hatch. Little black crows began to chip and push their way out of their shells. They chirped and called for their mother, but no crow came. Hawk looked down at them tenderly and said, "I will care for you, little ones," and she flew about to find food for them and when she returned she watched over them. Day after day, she fed them and looked after them.

The tiny crows grew bigger with Hawk's food and care. Their beautiful black feathers grew glossy and their wings grew strong. Still Hawk cared for them and fed them well.

Carefree Crow was flying over her old home on the hillside one day and spotted the nest she had left so long ago. "Perhaps I should return to it," she thought. As she approached the nest, she saw Hawk taking care of the little crows. "How dare you, Hawk!" screeched Crow, swooping down to the nest. "What's wrong?" asked Hawk, quite surprised. "Don't you know? I want my little crows back! They're mine!" screamed the very excited Crow.

Hawk ruffled her feathers and for a moment, was silent. Then she spoke softly, but firmly. "It is true, you laid the eggs. I see now that they were yours. But you flew off and left them, untended and unguarded. Anything could have happened to those poor little eggs. But I saw them and came to sit on the nest. For days I did not leave them. For days I did not eat a thing. When they hatched, I worked hard to find them food so that they would grow strong. It is I who have cared for them. It is I who will keep them!"

"I want them back!" screeched Crow once more.

"You may not have them," said Hawk. "Where were you when they needed warmth? Where were you when they were hungry? It is too late for you to come back now. They will stay with me."

"Well then," snapped Crow, "I will go to the King of the Birds and see what he has to say about this!"

"A fine idea," Hawk agreed, and off they went to see Eagle.

When they had told Eagle the story, Eagle asked, "Why did you leave your nest, Crow?"

Crow said nothing. Eagle turned to Hawk. "And how did you, Hawk, come upon the eggs?" asked Eagle.

"I was out flying one day when I saw a nest full of eggs with no one sitting on it. I waited to see if someone would come, but no one came at all," replied Hawk.

"But I laid those eggs!" cried Crow.

"Yes, but you did not care for them. It was I who sat on the eggs. It was I who hatched them and it was I who fed the little birds," said Hawk.

"But I am their mother! Just ask them. Go on and ask the little ones who their mother is!" said crow.

"Well," said Eagle turning to the baby birds, "who is your mother then?"

All together the little birds chirped, "Hawk is the only bird we call mother."

"No, I am your real mother," protested Crow.

But the little birds chorused, "You left us. Hawk stayed to hatch us and feed us. She is the only mother we know."

And so, it was settled. The little crows would stay with Hawk and not with Crow. And that is how precious things are lost when they are neglected.

Christianity

Responsibility is Rewarded

. . . the Kingdom of Heaven can be illustrated by the story of a man going into another country, who called together his servants and loaned them money to invest for him while he was gone.

He gave $5,000 to one, $2,000 to another, and $1,000 to the last—dividing it in proportion to their abilities—and then left on his trip. The man who received the $5,000 began immediately to buy and sell with it and soon earned another $5,000. The man with $2,000 went right to work, too, and earned another $2,000.

But the man who received the $1,000 dug a hole in the ground and hid the money for safekeeping.

After a long time, their master returned from his trip and called them to him to account for his money. The man to whom he had entrusted $5,000 brought him $10,000.

His master praised him for good work. "You have been faithful to me in handling this small amount," he told him. "So now I will give you many more responsibilities. Begin the joyous tasks I have assigned to you."

Next came the man who had received the $2,000, with the report, "Sir, you gave me $2,000 to use, and I have doubled it."

"Good work," his master said. "You are a good and faithful servant. You have been faithful over this small amount, so now I will give you much more."

Then the man with the $1,000 came and said, "Sir, I knew you were a hard man, and I was afraid you would rob me of what I earned, so I hid your money in the earth and here it is!"

But his master replied, "Wicked man! Lazy slave! Since you knew I would demand your profit, you should at least have put my money into the bank so I could have some interest. Take the money from this man and give it to the man with the $10,000. For the man who uses well what he is given shall be given more, and he shall have abundance. But from the man who is unfaithful, even what little responsibility he has shall be taken from him."

– Bible, Matthew 25:14-30

PROVERBS AND MAXIMS

If everyone sweeps in front of his own front door, all the world would be clean.

**What is popular is not always right.
What is right is not always popular.**

Ideas don't work unless we do.

Whenever you are to do a thing, though it can never be known but to yourself, ask yourself how you would act were all the world looking at you, and act accordingly.
– Thomas Jefferson

"Qui non est hodie, cras minus aptus erit."
(He who is not ready today will be even less so tomorrow.)
– Ovid

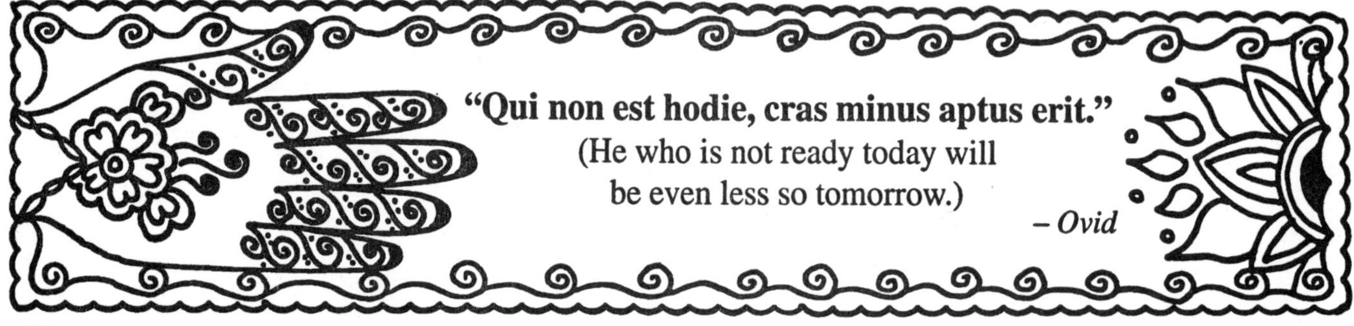

HEROES AND HEROINES

EDDIE AIKAU (1946–1978)

Born in Kahului, Maui, Eddie is probably best known as a big wave surfer, but his strength of character and his willingness to sacrifice for others will be his enduring tribute. As a lifeguard, he risked his life to save over a thousand people during a nine year period. As a member of the 1978 Hokulea crew, he gave his life in an heroic attempt to rescue the crew. Eddie was fearless in surfing the big waves of Waimea; regularly challenging waves over 20 feet, and on November 19, 1967 he caught a 35 foot monster at Waimea Bay. Whether he was surfing, lifeguarding, playing music or being with his family, his life had an unique focus and intensity. Before anyone had to ask for a volunteer to paddle for land when the Hokulea capsized, Eddie was untying the surfboard. "Eddie would go."

NELLIE BLY (1867–1922)

Born as Elizabeth Cochrane in a small town in Pennsylvania, a small girl with older brothers, she quickly learned how to survive with bravery and daring. She and her mother moved to Pittsburgh after her father died. Nellie decided she wanted to be a writer. She responded to a newspaper editorial critical of women's rights, won the respect of the editor and was hired as a reporter. Unable to use her name, she chose a name from a popular Stephen Foster song, Nellie Bly. She became well-known for her first-hand accounts of social inequity. She went into the slums, factories, hospitals, orphanages and prisons, exposing the terrible conditions. In New York City, working on the staff of the "World" for Joseph Pulitzer, she wrote such a devastating article about Blackwell's Island, the city's mental hospital, that it caused immediate reform and improvements.

THOMAS JEFFERSON (1743–1826)

Born at Shadwell, a tobacco plantation in Virginia, Thomas Jefferson was a member of one of Virginia's most distinguished families. He studied to become a lawyer, but practiced only a few years before entering politics. He became active in efforts to separate the colonies from English domination; and when he was elected as a delegate to the Second Continental Congress, he became the primary author of the Declaration of Independence. In 1800, he was elected as the third president of the United States. His accomplishments included efforts to reorganize the courts of law, to establish a system of public education, and to guarantee religious freedom. His skills in business, farming, inventory, language, architecture, education, government, and community planning made him an integral leader in the design of the United States.

ELEANOR ROOSEVELT (1884–1962)

Born in New York City, her father was Elliott Roosevelt, the younger brother of Theodore Roosevelt. Eleanor led a very troubled childhood; both her parents died while she was young (her father was an alcoholic and her mother was neurotic, preoccupied with social life and embarrassed at Eleanor's homeliness), and she went to live with her maternal grandmother. Convinced she would never marry, Eleanor plunged into social work. In 1905 she married her cousin, Franklin Delano Roosevelt. As a president's wife, she was quite independent and continued her interests in social service and modeled civic and national responsibility. After her husband's death, she served on the United Nations Commission on Human Rights and was instrumental in the completion of the Universal Declaration of Human Rights, which was adopted by the United Nations in 1948. She also worked with President Kennedy as an advisor for the Peace Corps and chair of the President's Commission on the Status of Women.

HARRY S. TRUMAN (1884–1972)

Born on a farm in Lamar, Missouri, he started as a farmer, but following service in the army during World War I, Harry became a partner in a men's clothing store. When the business failed, he turned to politics and became a county commissioner. In 1934, he was elected to the Senate and earned a reputation as a person of integrity as a special investigator of the national defense program. Supported by the conservatives, he replaced Wallace as Vice President and became President when FDR died in 1945. His first responsibility was to preside over the end of World War II as he authorized the dropping of the first atomic bomb on Hiroshima, Japan. His tough decisions guided America through some difficult years. Never shirking his duties and always accepting full responsibility for his decisions, he had a sign on his desk that read, "The buck stops here."

BOOKER T. WASHINGTON (1856–1915)

Born in Franklin County, Virginia as Booker Taliaferro (The Washington was later added) and a slave, he and his family were liberated by the Union Army in 1865. In return for being allowed a few hours of school each afternoon, his stepfather forced him to work in a salt mine in the morning and evenings. At age 16, he left home for Hampton Institute, proved himself to be an excellent student with scrupulous work habits and graduated 1876. He taught in a rural school for two years and joined the faculty at Hampton Institute where he supervised 100 Native Americans who had been admitted. In 1881, he was appointed to the task of founding Tuskegee Institute, a school for blacks. Under his leadership it became an important force in black education and he served as president until his death in 1915. In 1895, Washington gave his famous "Atlanta Compromise" speech where he renounced agitation and protest in favor of improving job skills and usefulness. Outwardly conciliatory, Washington secretly financed and encouraged attempts and lawsuits to block southern movers to disfranchise and segregate blacks.

PUT RESPONSIBILITY INTO ACTION

- Clean your room without being asked.
- Throw away your trash and pick up some litter.
- Practice self-control when you feel angry.
- Clean up your area after lunch and encourage your friend to do the same.
- Follow through on all assignments at school and chores at home.
- Do your chores at home without being asked.
- Look for something extra to do at home or in your community.
- Organize a park clean-up.
- Keep a promise.
- Express your anger with appropriate words and actions.
- Follow through on commitments to organizations that you join; clubs, sports teams, committees.
- Do some volunteer work in the community.

COMMUNITY SERVICE IDEAS

- Clean up your "own back yard" by collecting rubbish and recycling items around the school and home.

- Organize a graffiti clean-up party.

- Volunteer at a local Community Center helping elementary students with recreation, crafts, and other activities.

- Sponsor a canned food drive at your school. Take the food to a local soup kitchen and help feed the needy.

- Make informational posters encouraging members of your community to recycle. Provide the address and phone number of recycling services available in your area.

- Find an open area on your school grounds and plant a tree.

- Read your local paper and find a family or individual in need. (i.e. Victims of natural disasters, house fires, robbery, etc.) Provide them with food, clothing, or a collection of money from students in your school.

BOOKS ON RESPONSIBILITY

Horton Hatches the Egg. Dr. Seuss. New York: Random House, 1940.

The Book of Virtues. William J. Bennett, ed. New York: Simon and Schuster, 1993.

"The Boy and the Nuts" – p. 46
"Boy Wanted" – p. 78
"The Boy We Want" – p. 196
"The Declaration of Independence" – p. 251
"Etiquette in a Nutshell" – p. 201
"For Want of a Horseshoe Nail" – p. 198
"The Golden Touch" – p. 68
"The Goose that Laid the Golden Eggs" – p. 47
"Icarus and Daedalus" – p. 211
"If You Were" – p. 207
"King Alfred and the Cakes" – p. 196
"Let dogs Delight to Bark and Bite" – p. 37
"The Lovable Child" – p. 28
"Our Lips and Ears" – p. 44
"Please" – p. 24
"Rebecca" – p. 191
"St. George and the Dragon" – p. 192
"Sir Walter Raleigh" – p. 200
"Table Rules for Little Folks" – p. 42
"The Three Little Kittens" – p. 188
"Which Loved Best" – p. 204

November

Compassion

SUPPORTIVE VALUES

Service • Generosity

DEFINITIONS

The desire to ease others' suffering.

Compassion is a sympathetic awareness of another's distress combined with a desire to alleviate it. Even stronger than the word *sympathetic* is the word *empathetic,* which requires us to walk in another's shoes, truly striving to understand the plight of the less fortunate and seek ways to help. The words of the 14th Dalai Lama expand on this definition: ". . . each of us has responsibility for all humankind. It is time for us to think of other people as true brothers and sisters and to be concerned with their welfare, with lessening their suffering . . . we should think more about the future and benefit of all humanity."

Service and **Generosity** are ways in which we can demonstrate our compassion for others. Service is a contribution of time for the benefit of others. Generosity suggests giving freely and liberally of that which we have without expecting anything in return. Kahlil Gibran writes of the difference between service and generosity, "You give but little when you give of your possessions. It is when you give of yourself that you truly give."

PURPOSE

Students often recognize the plight of the homeless and hungry in their city and in the world. Amazingly, these are the same students who can be so callous toward each other and from whom critical remarks and cruel actions toward those with differences abound. Recalling our first month's emphasis on respect, along with partner values of acceptance and kindness, we can see how compassion connects. By putting the values of compassion and acceptance into action we can enable our students to help the child who is having a difficult time making friends and be of service by offering friendship. We can seek ways in which we can be of service in our classes: by volunteering to help, in our homes; by being helpful beyond our chores, in our schools; by doing litter clean-ups, taking care of our areas of play and study, in our communities; by contributing to needy causes, in our state, country, and world; by being aware of those less fortunate and finding ways to assist those outside of our personal world.

Compassion — November

Day One: Discuss the meaning of the word compassion.	**Day Two:** Kahlil Gibran, a famous writer, wrote "you give but little when you give of your possessions. It is when you give of yourself that you truly give". Have you given of yourself today?	**Day Three:** Think of ways teachers in your school show compassion for their students. Draw or paint a picture to show a special way a teacher shows compassion.	**Day Four:** Interview one of your classmates about their definition of compassion. Record the conversation.	**Day Five:** Compare and contrast your own understanding of the meaning of compassion with the classmate you interviewed.
Day Six: Plan a "day of caring" for your class. Work together as a group to 1) set aside the day 2) make a "menu of activities" from which class members can choose to carry out 3) appoint committees and define committee responsibilities.	**Day Seven:** Continue your plans from yesterday. The day of caring could focus on 1) the school environment 2) acts of random kindness to each other 3) honor and attention for school helpers or something unique to your class. Plan carefully to use your resources in a compassionate manner.	**Day Eight:** Assemble necessary supplies for your day of caring. Make posters, banners or awards if needed. Prepare the agenda for the day.	**Day Nine:** Carry out your "day of caring" with joy and thanksgiving!	**Day Ten:** Prepare a journal entry to reflect on the "day of caring" and its meaning to you.
Day Eleven: What images represent compassion? Make a list with your class and then choose one to draw.	**Day Twelve:** Some people believe that young people of today show less interest in and compassion for fellow human beings than did their parents and grandparents when they were the same age. Agree or disagree with this belief and give good reasons for your position.	**Day Thirteen:** Think of one specific thing someone in your family did during the past week to show compassion for you. Reflect on the consequences of this act and ask yourself how it made a difference in your feelings about yourself.	**Day Fourteen:** Find in the library and read the story of Saint Francis of Assisi and his compassion for all living things, especially the birds. Consider the many opportunities boys and girls of your age have to show compassion for animals in your own community. List some of the things you could do.	**Day Fifteen:** Make a classroom mural or create individual drawings or displays to illustrate the topic "care and concern for all creatures great and small."
Day Sixteen: Aesop, a great story teller who lived a long time ago, often used fables to illustrate the benefits of acts of kindness and compassion. Many of his stories feature animals as characters. Read and act out his fable of the lion and the mouse which illustrates an act of compassion returned in a surprising way.	**Day Seventeen:** Tell about a time when you felt true compassion for another person and you couldn't think of a way to help. How did you feel? If the same situation occurred again today, do you think you would behave differently?	**Day Eighteen:** Name and describe the person of your acquaintance who you consider to be the most compassionate person you know.	**Day Nineteen:** Make a list of things members of your class can do to show true compassion for less fortunate members of your community.	**Day Twenty:** Reflect on what embracing compassion as a life long value means to you personally.

COMPASSION IN OTHER LANGUAGES

Chinese	*ren*	perfect virtue; free from selfishness; the ideal of Confucius (the inner love for men which prompts to just deeds); benevolence; charity; humility
French	*la compassion*	pity; the feelings inspired by the misfortune of others
German	*mitgefhl*	compassion, sympathy
Hawaiian	*lokomaika'i*	kind, humane, gracious, benevolent oko – within, inside maika'i – goodness, righteousness
Japanese	*jin*	compassion
Korean	*yun min*	commiseration
Latin	*misericodia*	suffering together with another cum – together with pati – to suffer
Spanish	*compasión*	compassion, pity, sympathy
Tagalog	*pakikiramay*	feel sympathy and act in charity on behalf of someone in need

DISCUSSION QUESTIONS

- Why should we be compassionate toward others?
- For whom should we feel compassionate?
- How can we show compassion for someone?
- How do you feel when a member of your family is sick or having a terrible day? Do you look for ways to help them and maybe cheer them up?
- What are some of the things you do around the house to help life go smoothly? Do you always do this without being asked?
- Do you ever wish you could do something for other people in the world who need help?
- Can you think of some times when people need help?
- What are some of the events around the world that make you sad?
- What are some things we can do which help us deal with this kind of sadness?
- Is there anything we can do to help the people caught up in the events which cause human suffering?
- What can we do if there is not a specific way to help them directly?
- Have you ever volunteered to work on a service project? What kind of work did you do? Who and how did it help? How did it make you feel to volunteer?
- Have you ever given any of your treasured belongings to someone? How did giving away something you treasured make you feel?
- Have you ever contributed money you have earned yourself?

STORIES AND THOUGHTS FROM SPIRITUAL TRADITIONS

Hinduism

The true "Hindu" is that person who, on seeing violence perpetrated against any living thing ("hinsa"), experiences the suffering ("dukha") as if it was his own. – *Tradition*

When there is attachment to desires, there is pain.
Renunciation of attachments will lead to non-attachment.
Non-attachment will lead to love.
Love will lead to compassion. – *Tradition*

Rare are those who appreciate the merits of others.
Rare are those who hold the poor in affection.
Rare are those who remain calm in the battle, and
Rare are those who are distressed at the grief of others. – *Tradition*

Buddhism

Compassion is the wish to relieve the sufferings of living beings. Boundless compassion is the wish to relieve the sufferings of infinite living beings without exception.

Zen Buddhism

It isn't only upon the cultivation of such love and desire for universal salvation that all human beings will be equally able to share in the benefits of science and technology in the great, harmonious unity of this one world.

Christianity

"Be compassionate as your God is compassionate." *– Bible, Luke 6:36*

"When Jesus saw the crowds, he had compassion for them, because they were harassed and helpless, like sheep without a shepherd." *– Bible, Matthew 9:36*

"Put on then, as God's chosen people, compassion, kindness, lowliness, meekness and patience." *– Bible, Colossians 3:12*

The Parable of the Good Samaritan

One day an expert on Moses' laws came to test Jesus' orthodoxy by asking him this question: "Teacher, what does a man need to do to live forever in heaven?"

Jesus replied, "What does Moses' law say about it?"

"It says," he replied, "that you must love the Lord your God with all your heart, and with all your soul, and with all your strength, and with all your mind. And you must love your neighbor just as much as you love yourself."

"Right!" Jesus told him. "Do this and you shall live!"

The man wanted to justify his lack of love for some kinds of people, so he asked, "Which neighbors?"

Jesus replied with an illustration: "A Jew going on a trip from Jerusalem to Jericho was attacked by bandits. They stripped him of his clothes and money and beat him up and left him lying half dead beside the road.

By chance a Jewish priest came along; and when he saw the man lying there, he crossed to the other side of the road and passed him by. A Jewish Temple assistant walked over and looked at him lying there, but then went on.

But a despised Samaritan came along, and when he saw him, he felt deep pity. Kneeling beside him, the Samaritan soothed his wounds with medicine and bandaged them. Then he put the man on his donkey and walked along beside him till they came to an inn, where he nursed him through the night. The next day he handed the innkeeper two twenty-dollar bills and told him to take care of the man. 'If his bill runs higher than that,' he said, 'I'll pay the difference the next time I am here.'

Now which of these three would you say was a neighbor to the bandits' victim?"

The man replied, "The one who showed him some pity."

"Yes," Jesus said, "now go and do the same."

– Bible, Luke 10: 25-37

Casting the First Stone

Jesus was at the Temple. A crowd soon gathered, and he sat down and talked to them. As he was speaking, the Jewish leaders and Pharisees brought a woman caught in adultery and placed her out in front of the staring crowd.

"Teacher," they said to Jesus, "this woman was caught in the very act of adultery. Moses' law says to kill her. What about it?"

They were trying to trap him into saying something they could use against him, but Jesus stooped down and wrote in the dust with his finger. They kept demanding an answer, so he stood up again and said, "All right, hurl the stones at her until she dies. But only he who never sinned may throw the first!"

Then he stooped down again and wrote some more in the dust. And the Jewish leaders slipped away one by one, beginning with the eldest, until only Jesus was left in front of the crowd with the woman.

Then Jesus stood up again and said to her, "Where are your accusers? Didn't even one of them condemn you?"

"No, sir," she said.

And Jesus said, "Neither do I. Go and sin no more."

– Bible, John 8:1-11

Islam

The Messenger of Allah said: 'O Women of the Faithful, do not think it is a little thing which you give to your neighbour even if it is a small part of the leg of a goat.' (Abu Dawud included the addition:) 'Give gifts to each other for surely gifts take away ill feeling from the heart.'

321: Hadith
Bukhari: Book of Good Manners
– The Essential Teachings of Islam p. 207

The people of the Prophet's house killed a goat. Then they gave way portions to the poor, so that there remained only a portion thereof. The Prophet asked, 'What remains thereof?' They said, 'Nothing but the shoulder.' The Prophet said, 'Nay, all of it remains except its shoulder, for the reward thereof is eternal.'

– Selections from Mishkat-ul-masabi [110] p. 29

Chinese

Once when Yen Hui and Tzu-lu were waiting upon him the Master said, "Suppose each of you were to tell his wish." Tzu-lu said, "I should like to have carriages and horses, clothes and fur rugs, share them with my friends and feel no annoyance if they were returned to me the worse for wear." Yen Hui said, "I should never like to boast of my good qualities nor make a fuss about the trouble I take on behalf of others." Tzu-lu said, "A thing I would like is to hear the Master's wish." The Master said, "In dealing with the aged, to be of comfort to them; in dealing with friends, to be of good faith with them; in dealing with the young, to cherish them."

– The Analects, Book V

Act without lust of result; work without anxiety, taste without attachment to flavor; esteem small things great and few things many; repel violence with gentleness. Do great things while they are yet small, hard things while they are yet easy; for all things, how great or hard so ever, have a beginning when they are little and easy. The wise man considers even easy things hard, so that even hard things are easy to him.

– Tao Te Ching

The oceans and the rivers attract the streams by their skill in being lower than they; thus they are the masters thereof. So the Wise Man, to be above men, speaks lowly; and to proceed them, acts with humility.

So then do all men delight to honor him, and grow not weary of him. He contends not against any man; therefore no man is able to contend against him.

– Tao Te Ching

Judaism

If Not Higher

There was a newcomer who arrived in a village and was becoming acquainted with the people. The villagers were telling him about the rabbi who lived in their village who, every Friday, ascended to heaven. The newcomer was understandably skeptical. He found out where the rabbi lived and hid behind a tree near his house one Friday morning to watch him. He saw the rabbi leave his house on a wintry morning, chop down a tree and cut up the wood. Then he followed him to the house of an elderly woman who lived just outside the village, quietly leave the wood outside her house, then return home. The newcomer decided to stay and live in the village and ever after, when he would hear the villagers talk about their rabbi who ascended to heaven every Friday, he would reply, "if not higher."

Brothers

Once, long ago there lived a farmer named Seth who lived in the land of Israel. He had two sons, named Dan and Joel. When they were young, they followed Seth all about as he farmed the land, learning their tasks well. Every spring and every fall, they helped Seth plant the seeds. Then they would watch as the wheat grew and grew until it was over their heads.

When the wheat was finally ripe, Seth would harvest it with his sickle and the two brothers would help him to tie up the bushels, load them onto their donkey, and take them to be threshed. For many years, the boys and their father worked happily side by side. The boys grew taller and stronger as Seth grew older and tired from his labors. Finally, one day, Seth said to his sons, "You are not only good men and good farmers, but you have been very good sons. I am growing old and it is difficult for me to plow and plant. I no longer have the strength to harvest and thresh the wheat that we grow. I am weak and so very tired. My dear sons, I feel that soon I will die."

The two brothers were greatly saddened by their father's words, but listened as he continued. "I will divide my land in half so that when I am gone Dan will have one part, and Joel the other. I trust that you will always be as good to one another as you have been to me. I know that you shall always be friends and take good care of one another."

Soon after that, their dear father died. The land was divided in half and each of the brothers built a house on their part. Joel married a wonderful woman named Miriam. They were happy and over time, had three sons. As his family grew, Joel added rooms to their house, and his sons helped with all the work just as Joel and Dan had helped their father.

Dan, on the other hand, did not mary. He lived alone in a small house on his half of the land. He was happy to visit Joel and his family whenever he could.

One year, the rains did not fall as expected. The crops were poor and the harvest was very small. Neither Joel nor Dan had many bushels to thresh. One night, Joel was distressed and could not sleep. "What's the matter?" asked Miriam.

Joel sat up. "I am thinking about my poor brother," he said. "I am worried for he is all alone. We have our sons to help us and care for us when we are old. Dan is alone and has no one. He has so much less than we do. It is not fair that we should have the same amount of land and the same amount of wheat."

Miriam looked at him thoughtfully. "What will you do?"

Joel sat quietly for a moment then said, "I must take some of our wheat to my brother." So he dressed quickly and went out into the night. He loaded up his sleepy donkey with as much wheat as it could carry and set off for his brother's house. Once there, he silently placed all the wheat on his brother's threshing floor and returned home.

The very same night, Dan was also sleepless. He paced back and forth, thinking about his brother, Joel. "My dear brother has a wife and three sons to feed and care for. I have no one to care for but myself. It is not fair that we should have the same amount of land and the same amount of wheat. I must take some of my wheat to my brother!" he thought. So he went out into the night, loaded his donkey with wheat and took it to his brother's house. Silently, he unloaded the wheat and left it on his brother's threshing floor.

The next morning, when Joel saw all the wheat that there was on his threshing floor he was puzzled. "Why, there doesn't seem to be any less than there was yesterday. I must take some more to Dan tonight."

Dan was also surprised when he saw all the wheat on his threshing floor. "I must not have taken very much to my brother's house. I will be sure to take much more tonight."

That night, once again, Joel took wheat to Dan's house and Dan brought wheat to Joel's house. The next day, each brother had just as much wheat as the day before. Joel was very perplexed and spoke to his family about it. "Perhaps you need help," Miriam said. "Yes, tonight we will all help you," added the boys.

So that night Joel, Miriam and their sons loaded up the donkey with wheat and each carried as much as he could to Dan's house.

At the same time, Dan was starting out with a great load of wheat on his donkey and as much as he could carry in his arms to take to Joel.

The two brothers happened to meet halfway at the very spot which divided their father's property in half. As soon as they saw each other, they understood what had been happening. They did not need to speak to understand the concern that each had for the other. They dropped their bundles of wheat and embraced each other warmly.

Then, ever so sweetly, a voice swept around them singing, "How good it is for brothers to live in friendship."

Hundreds of years after that meeting, a city called Jerusalem had grown where Seth's farm had once been. In that city, a great king named Solomon had a temple built on the spot where the brothers met and embraced that night long ago. And there, at the temple, the same sweet voice has been heard to sing, "How good it is for brothers to live in friendship."

PROVERBS AND MAXIMS

The most human thing we can do is comfort the afflicted and afflict the comfortable.
– Clarence Darrow

The course of human history is determined, not by what happens in the skies, but by what takes place in our hearts. *– Sir Arthur Keith*

The one thing I know: the only ones among you who will be really happy are those who will have sought and found how to serve. *– Albert Schweitzer*

Never, if possible, lie down at night without being able to say: I have made one human being, at least, a little wiser, a little happier, or a little better this day. *– Charles Kingsley*

The test of our progress is not whether we add more to the abundance of those who have much; it is whether we provide enough for those who have too little.
– Franklin D. Roosevelt

HEROES AND HEROINES

JANE ADDAMS (1860–1935)

Born in Cedarville, Illinois, she was the youngest of five children. Her mother died, when Jane was still a baby, and she was taken care of by her sisters and brother. She became aware of poverty at age seven when she saw some poor children and she immediately announced that she wanted to build a house where they could come and play. After college, during a trip to Europe, she discovered a way to help the poor by living among them. She searched the slums of Chicago until she found a mansion in disrepair. She and a friend, Ellen Stan, fixed it up, moved in, and cared for the children of working mothers; thus Hull House was founded. In addition, she fought for child labor laws, safe working conditions, adult education, day nurseries, better housing and women's suffrage. She was awarded the Nobel Peace Prize in 1931.

PEARL SYDENSTRICKER BUCK (1892–1973)

Born in Hillsboro, West Virginia, while her parents were on a furlough from their mission field in China, she spent most of her first forty years in China, returning to the United States only for college and graduate studies. She married John Lossing Buck in 1917 and they lived in Nanking, China from 1921–34. She developed a deep compassion for the Chinese people and expressed this concern in many of her 85 novels, short stories and books of non-fiction. She was awarded the Nobel Prize for Literature in 1938, mostly because of her novel "The Good Earth" (1931), which also won her a Pulitzer Prize. She continued to promote social tolerance, was active in child welfare work (especially for disadvantaged Asian children) and founded Welcome House, an adoption agency for Asian-American children.

FATHER DAMIEN (1840–1889)

Born as Joseph de Veuster in Tremeloo, Belgium, he followed his brother to a contemplative monastery where he experienced a vision of St. Francis Xavier and was convinced that he should become a missionary. He substituted for his brother in a missionary party that was sailing for Hawaii in 1863. Upon arrival he was ordained a priest, to be known as Father Damien, and began regular work as a priest in a local parish. When he heard about the conditions of those suffering from Hansen's disease on Molokai, he decided they needed a resident priest. His ministry was a life of compassion, Christian humanism and service to people who had been separated and discarded from society. He served in Kalaupapa from 1873 until Hansen's disease claimed his life in 1889.

SWAMI VIVEKANANDA (1863–1902)

Born in India, he became India's first spiritual and cultural ambassador to the West. He presented a message to the World Parliament of Religions, held in Chicago in 1893, that focused on the unity of humankind and the harmony of religions. He wanted to create a bridge between the East and West by exchanging the message of India's ancient spirituality with scientific and industrial ideas of the West. He founded the Ramakrishna Order of India which is widely known for its charity; running hospitals and schools, rebuilding rural India and emergency relief work. He regarded the service of all people as the highest form of worship. He continued to teach the underlying truth of all religions, and the government of India declared his birthday a national holiday.

DALAI LAMA (1935–)

Born in the village of Takster, Tibet, he was known by the name of Lhamo. Following the death of the thirteenth Dalai Lama in 1933, and through a combination of prayer, tradition, and visions, monks were led to the home of a peasant family. There they were greeted by a two-year old boy, who immediately crawled into the lap of one of the monks and touched a rosary that had belonged to the Dalai Lama. After a series of tests, the boy was taken to Lhasa, the capital of Tibet, and formally installed as the Dalai Lama at age four. When the Chinese invaded Tibet in 1950, the Dalai Lama's life was in danger; he was forced to leave in 1959 and has been in exile since then. In spite of the atrocities committed by the Chinese on the Tibetan people, he has continued to speak of forgiveness, justice, and living together in harmony. When asked about his religion, Tibetan Buddhism, he replied, "My religion is kindness." He was awarded the Nobel Peace Prize in 1989.

MOTHER TERESA (1910–1997)

Born in Skopje, Yugoslavia, as Agnes Gonxha Bojaxhiu, she was the youngest of three children born to an Albanian couple. Her mother was a devout Catholic and took her young daughter with her on visits to the sick and the needy. After prayerful consideration, Agnes decided "to go out and give the life of Christ to the people;" she was twelve years old. She joined the sisters of Loreto and left for Calcutta in 1929. She taught high school until 1948, learning both Bengali and Hindi during this time. Agnes took her first vows of poverty, chastity and obedience in 1931, selected Teresa as her name and took her final vows in 1937. In 1946 she received a call to help the poor and formed the Missionaries of Charity in 1950. She added a fourth vow to the traditional three; "to give wholehearted, free service to the very poorest." Her work in the slums of Calcutta led to the awarding of the Nobel Peace Prize in 1979. She possessed a serene spirituality, a sense of joyful compassion, and a reverence for human life. She wrote, "We can do no great things, only small things with great love."

PUT COMPASSION INTO ACTION

- Be friendly to someone who needs a friend.
- Do helpful things at home without being asked.
- Be generous with your time and your belongings.
- Create and participate in a litter control program at your school.
- Pick up litter, wherever you are, instead of walking past it.
- Plan and participate in a canned food collection for a local charity.
- Look for ways to help in any situation without being asked.
- Put someone else's needs before your own.
- Look for ways to help someone in the community.
- Try to understand why a family member or friend is sad.
- Forgive someone who has hurt you.
- Talk with your family about the problems of the homeless. Find a way to help.
- Try to understand someone you disagree with or don't like.

COMMUNITY SERVICE IDEAS

- Recycle aluminum cans. Put the money earned into a local food bank.
- Collect food for a local food bank.
- Offer to help an elderly neighbor with their chores; get a friend to help you.
- Take a meal to someone who is ill.
- Visit a "shut-in" to add cheer to his or her day.
- Replace the signs about responsibility that you hung last month in your town with new signs reminding everyone to be compassionate toward each other.
- Write a letter or send a card of compassion to a victim of some recent tragedy.
- Create a school bulletin board where students and teachers can recognize people within the school who have demonstrated great compassion.
- Choose a historical figure who represents compassion. Write your own or find in the library a short play which tells about this person's compassionate acts. Perform the play for family or friends.

BOOKS ON COMPASSION

Alexander and the Terrible, Horrible, Very Bad, Mixed-Up Day. Judith Viorst. New York: Atheneum, 1972.

All I See. Cynthia Rylant. New York: Orchard Books, 1988.

Fly Away Home. Eve Bunting. New York: Clarion Books, 1991.

The Giving Tree. Shel Silverstein. New York: Harper & Row, 1964.

A Japanese Fairytale. Jane Ike. New York: F. Warne, 1982.

Shoebag. Mary Jones. New York: Scholastic, 1990.

Zoo. Anthony Brown. New York: Knopf, 1992.

The Book of Virtues. William J. Bennett, ed. New York: Simon and Schuster, 1993.

"A Child's Prayer" – p. 112

"Count That Day Lost" – p. 171

A Call to Character. Colin Greer and Herbert Kohl, eds. New York: Harper Collins Publishers, 1995.

"Black Beauty" – p. 323

"In Memory of Our Cat, Ralph" – p. 330

"A Raisin in the Sun" – p. 320

"The Wizard of Oz" – p. 219

The Moral Compass. William J. Bennett, ed. New York: Simon and Schuster, 1993.

"Abraham and the Old Man" – p. 735

"The Legend Beautiful" – p. 735

December

Faith

SUPPORTIVE VALUES

Hope • Trust

DEFINITIONS

Belief in and loyalty to a god, person, idea or something which cannot be proven.

Faith is having complete allegiance to a person or an idea. It refers to a belief in God and belief in something for which there is no proof. Faith speaks of confidence and conviction; qualities of inner strength. In this way, faith refers to belief in oneself and the quality of fidelity to one's promises.

Hope is to cherish a desire with every expectation that it will be fulfilled; to long for something with the same expectation. It also refers to someone or something on which this expectation is centered.

Trust is the assured reliance on the character, ability, strength, or truth of someone or something. It refers to the placing of confidence, dependence, reliance, or hope in someone or something.

PURPOSE

Most lists of universal/democratic values would not include faith. However, we feel both an opportunity and obligation to include faith as one of the primary values. Now that we have established respect and responsibility as the two "umbrella" values and have added compassion as an emphasis of including others, we add faith as the value that will lead our students toward the transcendent qualities of life. Thus, we move from self to others and, then, to that which is beyond (and within) our human experience. As Americans we draw primarily from the rich Jewish and Christian traditions but, as people and citizens of a global community, we want students to learn from the wisdom of different cultures and other world faiths. We must learn to live with and embrace diversity.

Faith — December

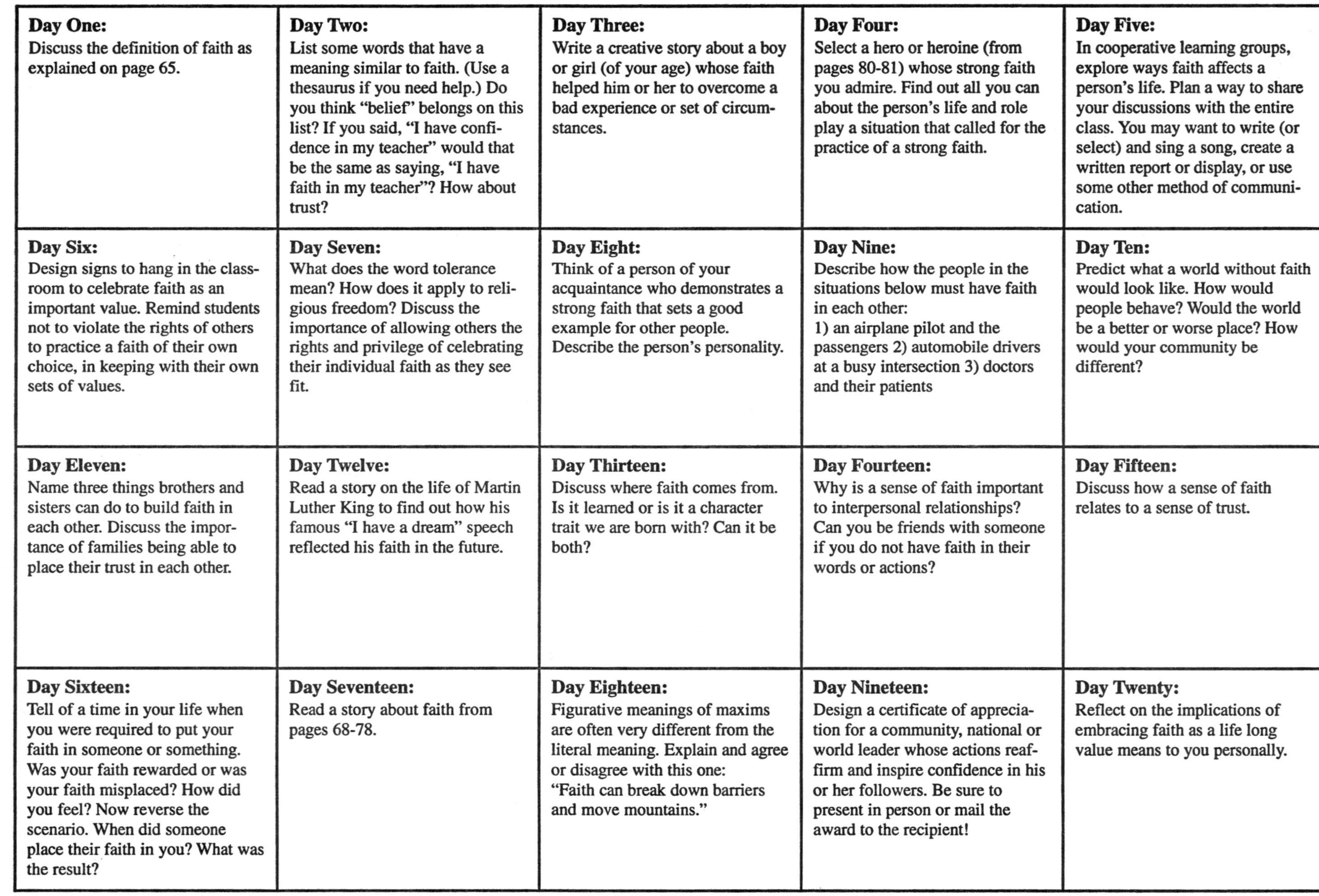

Day One:	Day Two:	Day Three:	Day Four:	Day Five:
Discuss the definition of faith as explained on page 65.	List some words that have a meaning similar to faith. (Use a thesaurus if you need help.) Do you think "belief" belongs on this list? If you said, "I have confidence in my teacher" would that be the same as saying, "I have faith in my teacher"? How about trust?	Write a creative story about a boy or girl (of your age) whose faith helped him or her to overcome a bad experience or set of circumstances.	Select a hero or heroine (from pages 80-81) whose strong faith you admire. Find out all you can about the person's life and role play a situation that called for the practice of a strong faith.	In cooperative learning groups, explore ways faith affects a person's life. Plan a way to share your discussions with the entire class. You may want to write (or select) and sing a song, create a written report or display, or use some other method of communication.
Day Six: Design signs to hang in the classroom to celebrate faith as an important value. Remind students not to violate the rights of others to practice a faith of their own choice, in keeping with their own sets of values.	**Day Seven:** What does the word tolerance mean? How does it apply to religious freedom? Discuss the importance of allowing others the rights and privilege of celebrating their individual faith as they see fit.	**Day Eight:** Think of a person of your acquaintance who demonstrates a strong faith that sets a good example for other people. Describe the person's personality.	**Day Nine:** Describe how the people in the situations below must have faith in each other: 1) an airplane pilot and the passengers 2) automobile drivers at a busy intersection 3) doctors and their patients	**Day Ten:** Predict what a world without faith would look like. How would people behave? Would the world be a better or worse place? How would your community be different?
Day Eleven: Name three things brothers and sisters can do to build faith in each other. Discuss the importance of families being able to place their trust in each other.	**Day Twelve:** Read a story on the life of Martin Luther King to find out how his famous "I have a dream" speech reflected his faith in the future.	**Day Thirteen:** Discuss where faith comes from. Is it learned or is it a character trait we are born with? Can it be both?	**Day Fourteen:** Why is a sense of faith important to interpersonal relationships? Can you be friends with someone if you do not have faith in their words or actions?	**Day Fifteen:** Discuss how a sense of faith relates to a sense of trust.
Day Sixteen: Tell of a time in your life when you were required to put your faith in someone or something. Was your faith rewarded or was your faith misplaced? How did you feel? Now reverse the scenario. When did someone place their faith in you? What was the result?	**Day Seventeen:** Read a story about faith from pages 68-78.	**Day Eighteen:** Figurative meanings of maxims are often very different from the literal meaning. Explain and agree or disagree with this one: "Faith can break down barriers and move mountains."	**Day Nineteen:** Design a certificate of appreciation for a community, national or world leader whose actions reaffirm and inspire confidence in his or her followers. Be sure to present in person or mail the award to the recipient!	**Day Twenty:** Reflect on the implications of embracing faith as a life long value means to you personally.

FAITH IN OTHER LANGUAGES

Chinese	*qian* *cheng*	to act with reverence; devout; sincere sincere; true; honest
French	*la foi*	faithfulness in fulfilling one's commitments, loyalty; confidence in something or someone; believing in God or a body of religious truths
German	*glaube*	faith, belief, credence, trust, religious faith, creed
Hawaiian	*mana'o'i'o*	"faith, confidence" (mana'o means "thought, idea, belief, opinion" and 'i'o means "true, genuine, significant, real")
Japanese	*seijitsu*	to make things you said happen and the house will be full of the treasure sei—make things you said happen jitsu—to fill up the house full of treasure
Korean	*shin nyum*	belief with confidence
Latin	*fides*	trust
Spanish	*fe*	faith, trust
Tagalog	*pananalig*	trust and believe in God or an idea without proof

DISCUSSION QUESTIONS

- What is something rather easy to have faith in? Love of family, future happiness, rising of the sun?

- What is something difficult? World peace, ending world hunger, cure for serious illness?

- Is a faith in others easy or difficult? Is it easy to have faith in yourself?

- How many religious faiths can you name?

- What areas of your life are helped or strengthened by faith?

- What are the obstacles to a strong faith?

- When do some people feel they need a faith in God? Sickness, personal challenge?

- What or who do you have faith in? Why?

- What does your faith have in common with other faiths?

STORIES AND THOUGHTS FROM SPIRITUAL TRADITIONS

Hinduism

Among those who are purified by their good deeds, there are four kinds of men who worship me: the world-weary, the seeker for knowledge, the seeker for happiness and the man of spiritual discrimination. The man of discrimination is the highest of these. He is continually united with me. He devotes himself to me always, and to no other. For I am very dear to the man, and he is dear to me.

Certainly, all these are noble: But the man of discrimination
I see as my very Self.
For he alone loves me
Because I am myself: The last and only goal
Of his devoted heart.
Through many a long life
His discrimination ripens: He makes me his refuge,
Knows that Brahman is all.
How rare are such great ones!

Men whose discrimination has been blunted by worldly desires, establish this or that ritual or cult and resort to various deities, according to the impulse of their inborn natures. But it does not matter what deity a devotee chooses to worship. If he has faith, I make his faith unwavering. Endowed with the faith I give him, he worships that deity, and gets from it everything he prays for. In reality, I alone am the giver.

– *Bhagavad Gita*

For he who turns to God his face, lifetimes of sufferings will be erased.

– *Ramcaritmanas*

"If the Lord were to consider all my deeds, then I would know no redemption for at least 70 million lifetimes. (But) the Lord doesn't pay attention to the faults of his devotees. He is the friend of the suffering and of most gentle nature."

– *Ramcaritmanas*

The whole reason one does spiritual practices is to come to the realization that on our own, we can accomplish nothing. It is only then that we can surrender our ego and open our hearts to God.

– *Swami Ramdas*

Buddhism

Faith is of three kinds: blind faith, reasoned faith, and clear faith. Blind faith is not recommended. Reasoned faith is confidence gained through sound reasoning. Clear faith is confidence gained through experience.

The Relic

Once upon a time in Tibet there was an old woman who was very religious. She had one son who was a trader, travelling back and forth from Tibet to India on business. The old woman was very keen on having a relic of the Buddha as the object of her devotions, so she asked her son to bring her a Buddha relic the next time he went to India.

The old woman's son travelled for six weeks by foot to India, buying and selling his wares along the way. After some months, he returned to Tibet. When he reached home, his mother asked him for the relic and was very sad when she found he had brought nothing.

The next year again the son travelled to India on business, and just as before, his mother asked him to bring a relic of the Buddha with him when he returned to Tibet. After some months, he returned home, again without the relic.

The next year, when he again set out for India, his mother said, "This time for sure you must remember to bring me a relic of the Buddha for my religious devotions. If you do not, I shall commit suicide when you return." After some months again, the son returned from his journey to India, but just as he was approaching his home, he realized that he had again forgotten his mother's request.

Fearing that his mother might indeed commit suicide if he returned home empty-handed for the third time, he decided he must take her something. Just at that moment, he saw a dog's tooth lying on the ground below him. Picking it up and dusting it off, he wrapped the dog's tooth in a beautiful silken cloth. When he reached home, he presented it to his mother, saying, "Here is the relic you requested—a tooth of the Buddha."

His mother, delighted, placed the tooth on the altar and began her religious devotions. From that day forth, the tooth emanated radiant, beautiful light in many colors that was seen by hundreds of people. Due to the old woman's faith, the tooth became an object of reverence that inspired religious devotion for miles around.

Christianity

"Remember the Sabbath day, to keep it holy."

– Bible, Exodus 20:8

"And I heard the voice of the Lord saying, 'Whom shall I send and who will go . . . for us?' Then I said, 'Here I am, send me.'"

– Bible, Isaiah 6:8

The Woman Who Touched Jesus

The leader of a local synagogue, whose name was Jairus, came and fell down before Jesus, pleading with him to heal his little daughter.

"She is at the point of death," he said in desperation. "Please come and place your hands on her and make her live."

Jesus went with him, and a crowd thronged behind. In the crowd was a woman who had been sick for twelve years with a hemorrhage. She had suffered much from many doctors through the years and had become poor from paying them, and was no better but, in fact, was worse. She had heard all about the wonderful miracles Jesus did, and that is why she came up behind him through the crowd and touched his clothes.

For she thought to herself, "If I can just touch his clothing, I will be healed." And sure enough, as soon as she had touched him, the bleeding stopped and she knew she was well!

Jesus realized at once that healing power had gone out from him, so he turned around in the crowd and asked, "Who touched my clothes?"

His disciples said to him, "All this crowd pressing around you, and you asked who touched you?"

But he kept on looking around to see who it was who had done it. Then the frightened woman, trembling at the realization of what had happened to her, came and fell at his feet and told him what she had done. And he said to her, "Daughter, your faith has made you well; go in peace, healed of your disease."

– Bible, Mark 5:22-34

Islam

There are three things by which any one who possess these in him shall taste the sweetness of faith, namely, whoever loves God and His apostle more than anything besides them; whoever loves a servant (of God) only for (the sake of) God; and whoever is averse to return to infidelity after that God has saved him from it even as he would be averse to be flung into the fire (of hell).

– *Selections from Mishkat-ul-masabi [211] p 49*
Ana, BU: MU: TI: NA.

Chinese

"The Good Man rests content with Goodness; he that is merely wise pursues Goodness in the belief that it pays to do so."

– *Confucius*

"Here is the mystery of Virtue: it creates all and nourishes all; it directs all, but without conscious control."

– *Lao Tzu*

We look at it and see it not, though it is Omnipresent;
and we name it the Root—balance.

We listen for it, and hear it not, though it is Omniscient;
and we name it the Silence.

We feel for it, and touch it not, though it is Omnipotent;
and we name it the Concealed.

These three Virtues have it; yet we cannot describe it as consisting of them;
but mingling them aright, we apprehend the One.

– *Tao Te Ching*

Hawaii

Faithful Friends in the Forest

Lono was the chief of the big island of Hawaii. He was excited about making a trip to the island of Kaua'i and seeing the famous Waimea Canyon, the many waterfalls, the beautiful forests and beaches. He told his servants to get his canoe and belongings ready for the journey. They obeyed his command but grumbled as they worked. Lono's servants did not like having to go all that way to a strange place with strange gods.

The chief was so happy about making the trip he was not aware of the unhappiness of his servants. As they neared the coast of Kaua'i he could not take his eyes off the beautiful green cliffs of the island. He encouraged his paddlers to pick up their pace, and as soon as the canoe landed on the beach he began asking people of Kaua'i, who had gathered to greet the strangers, where the canyon and the waterfalls were. He commanded his servants to tie up the canoe, bring his food and belongings, and follow him. He left the beach and began to hike at an eager and swift pace.

After a long time of climbing the trail he stopped to rest only to find that he was alone. When he looked back down the trail he saw only one man following after him. He realized in his haste he'd left all of his followers behind. He waited for the man and as he approached he saw that he was a stranger. "Who are you?" the chief asked. "I am Kapa'ihi of Kaua'i and I watched you land your canoe and then quickly leave it. Your followers watched you leave and then got back into the canoe when you were out of sight and paddled it back toward Hawaii. I thought you would need a guide and some food so I have brought some fish and poi. Let me serve you great chief."

"Those disloyal followers! They must be punished!" But as his eyes gazed at the beauty in the valley below him he was no longer angry. "Never mind them," he said, "I'm finally here on Kaua'i. Let's go see the sights I've longed to see." They climbed up the steep slopes for a long time and finally arrived at the edge of the canyon. He saw the stream which flowed far below them, it seemed so tiny next to the towering red walls of the canyon. He could see small white birds in the distance, they were the only moving sight for the viewer of such a glorious scene. Lono marveled at the breathtaking beauty of the canyon.

It was growing dark and a cool breeze came from the mountains and chilled the chief. Kapa'ihi gave him his own shoulder cape and led him to a cave which sheltered them from the wind. He knelt and served Lono the fish and poi and made a bed of dry grass, which he'd gathered, for them to sleep on.

Every day Lono and Kapa'ihi explored Kaua'i. They hiked over mountains, went into remote valleys and enjoyed the many waterfalls which plunged into fern embraced pools of fresh water where they could swim. They looked at the steep, green cliffs of the coast which rose straight up from the beach. They finished the fish and poi and then Kapa'ihi found banana, fern shoots, and pandanus fruit to feed them. They each wore a shoulder cape he made from leaves to protect them from the rain. Kapa'ihi always walked several steps behind the chief out of respect for his position and always served him his food on his knees.

One evening Lono realized that he had gone so many places and done so much with Kapa'ihi that he should no longer have him act as a servant toward him but rather as a friend and companion which he truly had become. He became so fond of this humble and thoughtful man that he was determined to have him honored when he returned to his island of Hawaii.

When the chief finally returned from Kaua'i he immediately punished all the men who had deserted him and made Kapa'ihi his trusted assistant. The others were jealous of this stranger's high rank and tried to convince Lono that Kapa'ihi was not trustworthy. Lono replied, "Together we have traveled the mountains and valleys of Kaua'i, Kapa'ihi and I, together we have seen waterfalls and walked in the rain, together we have seen the amazing canyon and steep, green cliffs. He was always beside me through our travels, loyal and faithful and you tell me he can't be trusted?" The jealous ones knew it was useless to say anything more.

After Kapa'ihi had served the chief for a long time on Hawaii he requested permission to return to Kaua'i to visit his family. Lono granted permission but asked Kapa'ihi to keep his trip brief for he was dependent on him for advice and companionship. Kapa'ihi returned to his home island. Soon after he heard rumors that Lono never wanted to see him again. The chief had heard stories from the jealous people about Kapa'ihi which he believed. Kapa'ihi did not believe that his dear friend would do this to him and he was saddened by these rumors. In his sadness he wrote a song recalling their time together traveling on Kaua'i and exploring the beauty of the island.

When he returned to Hawaii he was told by the guard that he was not allowed to enter the home of the high chief Lono, his friend. He was shocked and dismayed! The rumors were true. He slumped down beside the house and began to sing his song. Inside the chief heard the words of his friend and felt ashamed. Why had he believed the stories of others and doubted the faithfulness of his dear companion? He ran to the door and told the guard to bring Kapa'ihi into his home. The guard told him that Kapa'ihi had gone. As they looked toward the beach they saw him getting into his canoe and paddling away.

"Go after him and bring him back, quickly, go!" The guard obeyed, but later returned saying that Kapa'ihi said, "Give my love to your chief, but tell him that I cannot return because he has believed the lies of others and shut his door to me." Lono realized that he needed to apologize to Kapa'ihi himself, for he had been wrong about his friend and had treated him badly.

Lono ordered his double canoe to be readied and followed Kapa'ihi. Soon they came to Kohala and saw a man sitting on the beach with his head bent in sorrow. Lono realized it was his faithful friend and went to him. He softly began to chant the words of the song that Kapa'ihi had created about their journey together. Kapa'ihi looked up and greeted his chief with a smile. The two men embraced affectionately and Lono vowed to never let lies come between them again.

India

Faith, Devotions, and Resignation

A milkmaid used to supply milk to a Brahmin priest living on the other side of a river. Owing to the irregularities of the boat service, she could not supply him milk punctually every day. Once, being rebuked for her coming late, the poor woman said, "What can I do? I start early from my house, but have to wait for a long time at the riverbank for the boatman and the passengers." The priest said, "Woman! They cross the ocean of life by uttering the name of God, and can't you cross this little river?" The simple-hearted woman became very glad on learning this easy means of crossing the river. From the next day on the milk was always supplied in the morning.

One day the priest said to the woman, "How is it that you are no longer late?" She said, "I cross the river by uttering the name of the Lord as you told me to do, and I don't stand now in need of a boatman." The priest could not believe this and said, "Can you show me how you cross the river?" The woman took him with her and began to walk over the water. Looking behind, the woman saw the priest in a sad plight and said, "How is it, Sir, that you are uttering the name of God with your mouth, but at the same time with your hands you are trying to keep your cloth untouched by water? You do not fully rely on Him." Entire resignation and absolute faith in God are at the root of all miraculous deeds.

Judaism

The Precious Prayer

During Yom Kippur, Rabbi Isaac Luria was praying in a synagogue when an angel came and told him about a man whose words, when he prayed, reached the highest of heavens. The angel told him the name of the man and where he lived. When Yom Kippur was over, the rabbi made haste to find this man.

He searched the city for the man. First he went to the House of Study, then to the market, where he asked for information on the man with that name. He was told that the man lived in the mountains and was a poor farmer.

The rabbi set out for the mountains to find the farmer and was surprised when he found him that his house was just a poor hut. He was greeted by the farmer and invited into the hut. The rabbi asked him to tell him about his prayers. Surprised by the question, the man told the rabbi that he could not say prayers because he did not know how to read although he knew his alphabet.

Puzzled by this response, the rabbi asked the man what he did on Yom Kippur. The man replied that he had gone to the synagogue and had seen everyone praying. He felt heartbroken, so he recited the alphabet and asked that God take the letters and form them into a prayer which would rise like the scent of honeysuckle, for that was the sweetest scent he knew. The farmer said that he repeated this plea with all his strength over and over.

The rabbi understood what secret God had sent him to learn: that man sees only what is before his eyes, but God sees what is in the heart, which is what made the prayers of the farmer so precious.

Japanese

Jojofu

Long, long ago, there lived a fine young hunter named Takumi. Takumi hunted wild boar and deer in the mountains and kept about thirty hunting dogs, which he cared for dearly. He loved his dogs deeply; but of the thirty, there was one called Jojofu who was his favorite. She was not only the bravest, but the very smartest of the pack.

One day, Takumi set off with ten of his strongest dogs into the mountains. It was a good day for hunting. As usual, the dogs followed close behind Takumi as they climbed higher and higher into the woods—all but Jojofu. Takumi always let Jojofu remain at his side, as she feared nothing and could always signal Takumi against danger.

Takumi let Jojofu lead them through thick brush and over a rough path until they came to a grassy clearing. But rather than remain on the open grass where it would be easiest to walk, Jojofu darted immediately back into the dark woods. "Where are you taking us, silly dog? It is so much more difficult to make our way through the woods!"

But Jojofu continued to lead them into the trees, turning to bark an encouragement for them to follow. Takumi cried after her, "Jojofu! This is not the way! Come here!"

All at once, there was a great rumbling coming from the clearing behind them. Takumi turned to see huge boulders cascading down the hillside and tumbling on to the clearing they had just left. "A landslide," Takumi murmured. "We would have been buried there had it not been for Jojofu!" He called her to his side and said, "Forgive me for not trusting your eyes and ears, which are much sharper than my own."

The group moved on through thicker woods and a heavy gray mist hung over them, veiling their sight. Jojofu led them slowly and carefully as she felt for the safest trail. All of a sudden, she stopped. Takumi urged her on, but she would not budge. "We must continue, Jojofu, or we will not get to the hunting grounds before nightfall." Jojofu let out a sharp bark, then lay down at her master's feet, refusing to proceed. Impatient, Takumi called to one of his livelier dogs, Bakana. Bakana raced forward, bounding past Jojofu and Takumi into the heavy mist. Only seconds later did they hear a yelp and the sound of crashing stones and falling dirt. With fear and regret, Takumi picked up a long stick and felt his way through the mist. After only a few steps he felt where the path ended, and the ground dropped off suddenly at the edge of a treacherous cliff.

Takumi turned back to Jojofu and dropped to his knees. "Jojofu," he cried, "once again you have tried to lead me to safety. I promise I will never again lose faith in you whatever you do!"

By this time, the air had grown very crisp and night was falling, so Takumi decided to make camp. He built a large campfire and found a place to sleep in the broad branch of a tall tree. He knew he would be safe from the creatures in the forest if he were high off the ground, especially with Jojofu keeping guard below. So after a meal of fish and rice, he climbed up into his lofty bed and fell asleep.

A few hours later, a deep growl from Jojofu awoke Takumi. He rubbed the sleep from his eyes and looked down to see Jojofu staring up at him from below. Her eyes glared up at him through the darkness and she snarled viciously, baring her bright teeth.

"What's wrong, Jojofu? Can't you see it's only me up here? Now go to sleep, girl," Takumi called down to his dog.

With that, she lept up at the base of the tree, her front paws clawing at the bark, her eyes yellow with anger. Her lips curled back as she barked fiercely upward at Takumi. He saw the white froth at her mouth and became worried. "Could she have eaten a poisonous mushroom? What could have made her crazy like this?" Then, with great shock, he realized that none of the other dogs remained below. There was only Jojofu, gone wild, as Takumi had never seen her before. "Something is terribly wrong," thought Takumi, as Jojofu's rage seemed to build.

"She is mad!" thought Takumi, fearing for his own safety. Slowly, he drew out his sword, dreading what he thought he must do. The sword flashed in the moonlight, but Jojofu did not back away. Instead, she leapt higher and higher, getting closer to Takumi's branch with each bound. Afraid of her anger and strength, Takumi wondered whether he might have to kill his beloved companion in order to save himself. Then, he remembered the promise he had made at the cliff. He had said that no matter what, he would not lose faith in her. Even if she were mad, he would not turn against her. He slid his sword back into its sheath, took a deep breath, and jumped to the ground below.

In the same instant that he left his branch, Jojofu leapt high into the air and landed just where Takumi had made his bed. She snarled and clawed among the branches just above, then suddenly fell to the ground with a giant snake held between her powerful jaws. Takumi was terrified as Jojofu and the great beast thrashed about. Then, as if awakening suddenly from a nightmare, he drew his sword swiftly and killed the enormous snake.

He took Jojofu into his arms and cried, "Once more you have saved my life. I will trust you always, my beloved and faithful friend!" Just then, Jojofu broke out of Takumi's embrace and ran toward the lifeless serpent.

She sniffed at the snake's belly and began to bark and paw at it. "Is it still alive, girl?" Takumi asked nervously. Once again he drew his sword and struck at the creature's stomach. From the opening emerged all of Takumi's missing dogs. They ran to Jojofu, licking her face in gratitude.

Takumi never traveled without Jojofu beside him. Stories were told from village to village about the courageous hunter and his faithful companion who killed the huge serpent. Takumi told all he met of his trust in Jojofu, his eyes and ears.

PROVERBS AND MAXIMS

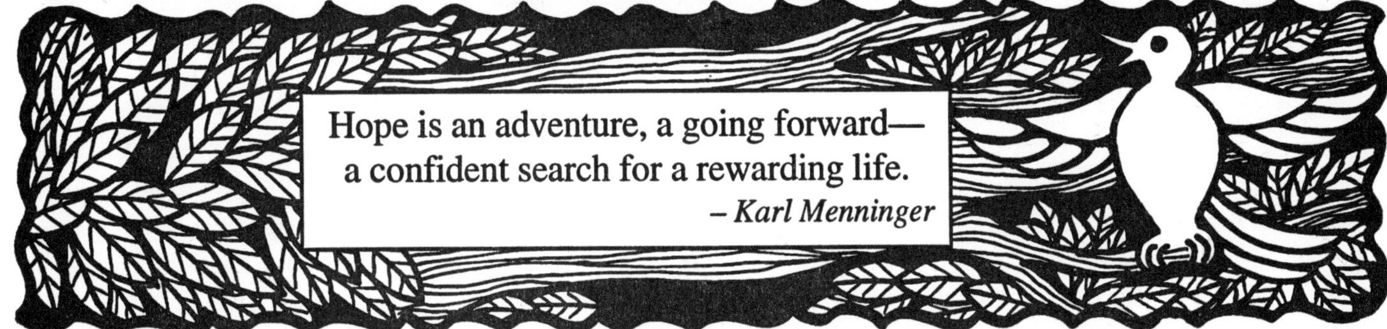

I'd hate to say my faith's a rock, but it's true. It is my strength; it gives me inner peace. Without my faith, I'd be in real bad shape. Faith gives a man hope, and hope is what life is all about. *– Tom Landry, NFL Coach*

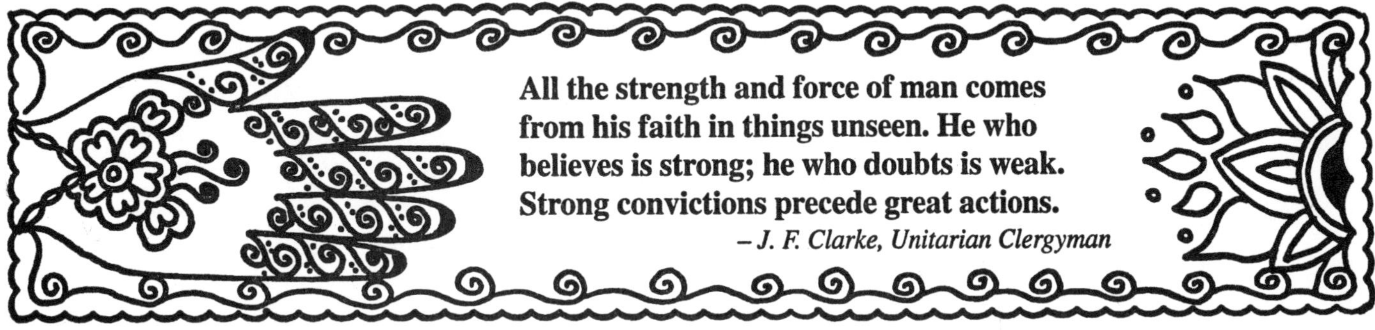

HEROES AND HEROINES

JESUS (c. 3 B.C.E.–30 C.E.)

He was born in Bethlehem, Israel of humble Jewish parents, his father a carpenter and his mother a peasant teenager. Jesus grew up in relative obscurity learning his father's trade. He entered the public eye when he appeared at the River Jordan where John the Baptist was proclaiming the coming of the Messiah and baptizing people in the river as symbol of hope and new beginnings. John recognized Jesus as this new religious leader and baptized him. Jesus soon after began a three year period of teaching and healing around Galilee. He choose twelve men to travel with him, and rather than teach in the synagogues he preferred hillsides and river banks where the poor people could gather around him. Quoting from the Jewish law and prophets, he gave an interpretation that lifted up a new commandment of love. He taught with stories and parables and unintentionally challenged the religious authorities. He was accused of disturbing the peace, brought before Jewish and Roman tribunals and executed by crucifixion. His followers stayed together, forming a Jewish sect that became Christianity.

BUDDHA (c. 566–486 B.C.E.)

Born in Kapilavastu, Nepal, where his father ruled the Sakya tribe of the Gautama clan, he led the sheltered life of a young prince. He was married at age 16 and had one son. Tormented by the mysteries of illness, old age, and death he decided to leave his home, his riches, and his title to search for the truth. At the age of 29, he left the palace and traveled as a homeless holy man. He followed the teachings of two yoga masters without success and lived as an extreme ascetic for six years. Close to death and meditating on the mysteries of death and rebirth, the secrets were revealed to him, and he felt freed from all passions and all spiritual blindness. He gave his first sermon near Barnes in which the Four Noble Truths were outlined. He spent the rest of his life teaching and created a new order of itinerant monks. Worn out with age and exhaustion, he stopped in a forest near Kusinagori and, lying down between two trees, died peacefully, entering perfect nirvana.

KOBO DAISHI-KUKAI (774–835 C.E.)

Born in what is now Zentsuji City, Mao Kukai, the third son of Saeki Yoshimichi, was so bright and gifted his parents expected him to go into government service, which was the most respected profession at that time. He started his studies at the university in Kyoto, but he was more interested in searching for ultimate truth. A Buddhist monk introduced him to a practice of meditation called Kokugo-gumonjiho. As a result, he chose Buddhism and the priesthood rather than Confucianism and government bureaucracy. At age 19, in a cave at Cape Muroto, he attained a stage of enlightenment through his practice of meditation and made his final declaration to Buddhism. At age 31 he went to China and studied with Abbot Huikeo, the 7th patriarch of Esoteric Buddhism, who recognized immediately that Kukai would be his successor. After three months of study, Kukai was ordained the 8th patriarch of Esoteric Buddhism, and his master instructed him to return to Japan and spread the teachings and increase the happiness of the people there. He is credited with the founding of Japanese Buddhism. There are 3,000 folk tales and legends about this man who called himself Priest Kukai. In 921 he was canonized as Kobo Daishi; Daishi means great saint and Kobo means to spread.

LAO TZU (Third Century B.C.E.)

Three hundred years before the time of Confucius, a unique collection of people distilled the oral and written tradition of a thousand years into a work known as the *Tao Te Ching*. They lived along the Yellow River and in the remote valleys of north central China and were the descendants of a people who had a very advanced culture. Over several hundred years they had developed extensive written literature and produced many original philosophical thinkers. Sometime during the third century B.C.E., these people wrote the poems of the *Tao Te Ching*. Since there is no identifiable author it was necessary to invent one. By the time the *Tao Te Ching* was put into form, legend had provided an author, Lao Tzu—the old one or the old philosopher. Perhaps, Lao Tzu is the pseudonym or pen name of an ancient philosopher who was one of those reclusive mystics. *Tao Te Ching* translates as "The Book of the Way and Its Virtue" and is the basis of Taoism or The Way.

MUHAMMAD (c. 570–632 C.E.)

Born in Mecca, Muhammad was raised by a grandfather and an uncle. They took him into the family business of caravan trade. It was on one of their trips that he met some Nestorian monks, one of whom (Bahira) foretold his destiny as a prophet. Muhammed later became dissatisfied with the polytheism that was prevalent during that time and was especially displeased with the way the Ka'bah was being used for the worship of pagan idols. He was attracted to the monotheistic ideas being spread by Jews and Christians. He began regular retreats to a mountain cave and practiced long hours of asceticism and meditation. It was during one of these times in the year 610 that he had a dream that a book had been written in his heart. The dream was accompanied by the angel Gabriel and Muhammad became accustomed to receiving messages from God. He revealed these messages to a few disciples and after three years of revelations he was ordered to begin his public career. He proved to be a capable military and political leader and soon enjoyed absolute power. The complete Revelation is written down in the Koran and is complimented by a record of his oral teachings in the Hadith. Together they provide the basis for the faith of Islam.

PUT FAITH INTO ACTION

- Spend some time in meditation or prayer.
- Read something spiritual or religious.
- Put your trust in someone.
- Don't give up!
- Find something you can believe in beyond yourself.
- Attend a worship service of a religion you do not practice.
- Make a list of ways that faith affects the way you live your life and the decisions you make.

COMMUNITY SERVICE IDEAS

- Collection of toys, clothes, games for a local holiday project.
- Make Christmas cards for children who are sick.
- Start an angel tree. Ask students to bring hats, scarves, and mittens to hang on the tree. Donate the gifts to the needy.
- Go Christmas caroling.
- Make banners or signs to hang up in your community to remind people of the importance of faith.
- Take a survey of people in your community to discover the role faith plays in people's everyday lives. Share what you discovered with your classmates.

BOOKS ON FAITH

Chicken Sunday. Patricia Polocco. New York: Philomel Books, 1992.
The Judge: An Untrue Tale. Harve Zemach. New York: Farrar, Strauss & Giroux, 1969.
St. Francis of Assisi. Nina Bawden. New York: Lothrop, Lee & Shepard Books, 1983.

The Book of Virtues. William J. Bennett, ed. New York: Simon and Schuster, 1993.
"The Captain's Daughter" – p. 760
"A Child's Prayer" – p. 744
"Deucalion and Pyrrha" – p. 775
"Going to Church" – p. 798
"Hanukkah Hymn" – p. 765
"The Honest Disciple" – p. 762
"I Never Saw a Moor" – p. 753
"The Kids Can't Take It If We Don't Give It" – p. 778
"Our Lady's Juggler" – p. 78
"St. Nicholas and the Golden Bars" – p. 763
"The Sermon to the Birds" – p. 761
"Sleep, My Babe" – p. 743
"We Understand So Little" – p. 774

Commitment

SUPPORTIVE VALUES

Loyalty • Effort

DEFINITIONS

A pledge to a person, worthy goal, or concept.

Commitment is the state of being committed to a worthy goal, issue or concept. With commitment comes a pledge to uphold a promise, to fulfill an obligation, or to complete an involvement.

Loyalty is the quality of being faithful to one's commitments. A person who is faithful to their nation is a loyal citizen; while faithfulness to a promise means being loyal to a vow, faithfulness to a person means being a loyal friend, and faithfulness to responsibilities describes loyal conduct. Dedication, duty and devotion are good words to use in conjunction with this value.

Effort is deliberate exertion of mental, physical or spiritual power. This is where hard work enters the process. There are individuals who have taken the Puritan Work Ethic to an extreme and neglected their family and personal health in favor of work. However, there are other times when a sustained expenditure of effort is necessary to accomplish a definite goal. A willingness to work hard to fulfill commitments is deserving of high priority.

PURPOSE

Inherent in every person's life are certain roles that entail particular responsibilities. Some of these roles are given to us, such as son or daughter, while others are chosen, such as musician or athlete. A consideration of the value of commitment will encourage our students to keep their word, keep trying until their goal is reached, and follow through on previously selected aspects of respect, responsibility, compassion, and faith.

Commitment — January

Day One: Discuss the meaning of commitment. Compare individual thoughts with the definitions provided on page 85.	**Day Two:** Use the discussion questions on page 88 to continue thinking and learning about commitment.	**Day Three:** Did you make a New Year's Resolution? If you did, share it with the class. It takes a lot of commitment to follow through on your resolution for an entire year. Try to make resolutions that are possible to keep and commit to keeping them.	**Day Four:** Commitment to a goal means hanging-in even when the goal seems impossible. Think of a time when you were committed to accomplishing a goal. (Learning to ride a bicycle or reading your first chapter book.) How did you feel when you finally reached that goal? Write a list of those feelings.	**Day Five:** Have you ever made a promise to do something for someone? (i.e. To keep your room clean or set the table for dinner.) That's a commitment! Write a short story or draw a picture which tells about sticking to your promise.
Day Six: Relationships take a lot of commitment to stay strong. Make a list of three people to whom you are willing to make a commitment to. Keep this list as a reminder of your commitment.	**Day Seven:** Choose a bookmark from page 98. Decorate it and cut it out. Then give it to a friend or relative as a sign of your commitment to maintaining the relationship.	**Day Eight:** Any type of long-term goal takes a lot of commitment. Choose and plan a community service project from page 100 .	**Day Nine:** Show your commitment as a class by following through with the service project.	**Day Ten:** Discuss your service project and determine if it was as successful as it could have been. Were all members of the class committed to the project? What would you do differently if you were to plan and carry out another class service project?
Day Eleven: Read a story about commitment from the selection on pages 89-97. Discuss what the story had to teach about the value of commitment?	**Day Twelve:** Create and present an award to someone you know who has followed through on an important commitment.	**Day Thirteen:** Rate on a scale from one (the easiest) to ten (the hardest) these acts of commitment. 1) Getting an A on your next test 2) Turning in all your homework assignments on time 3) Making your bed every morning for a week 4) Telling your friends the truth 5) Learning to play a new computer game.	**Day Fourteen:** When you get a pet, you must make a commitment to care for it. That is because pets are completely dependent on their owners for everything! Pretend you are getting a new pet. Write a list of things you will need to fulfill your commitment to properly care for it.	**Day Fifteen:** Is there something in your life that you would like to change for the better? Write down a list and then choose the one that is the most realistic and you feel you have the most commitment to. (i.e. Riding a bike, reading your first chapter book, etc.)
Day Sixteen: Meet with a partner to compare your lists from yesterday. Then join a class discussion to determine three things your class as a whole could commit to making changes for the better.	**Day Seventeen:** Team sports rely on each player's individual commitment to play his or her best. Team effort is key to a team success. Choose a team sport to play to understand team commitment.	**Day Eighteen:** Read about the heroes and heroines of commitment on page 99. Discuss how each person was rewarded by his or her commitment.	**Day Nineteen:** Make a banner or poster to post in the school cafeteria or library to remind students and visitors to the school of the importance of commitment to doing one's best every day.	**Day Twenty:** Reflect on the lessons of commitment that you have learned this month. Make a commitment to embrace these lessons throughout your life.

COMMITMENT IN OTHER LANGUAGES

Chinese	*heng*	constant, regular, continually, persevering
	xin	heart; the moral nature; the mind; the affections; intention
French	*l'engagement*	commit oneself to something or someone by means of a promise or contract; a decision to get publicly involved in social or political problems
German	*verpflichtung*	obligation, duty, commitment
Hawaiian	*kupa'a*	steadfast, firm, constant, immovable (ku means "to stand" and pa'a means "firm solid")
Japanese	*chikai*	to promise with words
Korean	*yak sok*	pledge
Latin	*pignus*	commitment from Latin "cum" (together with) + "mittere" (to send, give over) (something given over with another, a reciprocation)
Spanish	*compromiso*	commitment, obligation, duty
Tagalog	*panata*	promise, pledge or vow; promising to fulfill a certain duty with religious devotion

DISCUSSION QUESTIONS

- Why is it important to keep a promise? Share examples of promises that were made, how it may have been difficult to keep your word, and the results of keeping and breaking promises.
- What happens when we don't follow through on our responsibilities?
- Do you expect your family members and your friends to do what they say they'll do? Do you have the same expectation of yourself?
- Are you able to keep working on something until you get it done? Even when you're tired or don't feel like it?
- Why is it important to try hard to always do your best?
- What are some of the pledges of commitment that people make?(scouts, politicians, judges, doctors, class officers)
- Why is their commitment so important? What kind of commitments do people make to each other? (friendship, marriage)
- What are the signs of loyalty to: our nation? A friend? Our responsibilities? A promise?
- Would we be described as loyal or committed? Why or why not? Share an example of a promise you've made and kept. Was it difficult or easy? Why?
- Do you choose friends based on how trustworthy they are?
- Is it possible to enjoy hard work? Is it really hard or is concentration made easy because you enjoy it? Is it possible to make all hard work enjoyable?

STORIES AND THOUGHTS FROM SPIRITUAL TRADITIONS

Hinduism

Never promise anything unless you are willing to die in order to fulfill it.

– Tradition

One who takes a virtuous vow has the strength of seven generations to help him succeed. One who breaks a vow brings ill fortune on seven generations.

– Tradition

Buddhism

Commitment, or joyful effort, overcomes all obstacles, especially laziness and procrastination.

Chinese

"In your promises cleave to what is right, and you will be able to fulfill your word. In your obeisances cleave to ritual, and you will keep dishonor at bay."

– Confucius

Hawaii

Punia

In ancient times there lived an elderly couple in Kohala on the Big Island, who had no children. Leimakani, the husband, was a sweet potato farmer and lived with his wife Hina. One day Hina began to have a craving for coconut which was forbidden for women to eat. Leimakani was careful in his observance of the restrictions of the gods and knew he must not try to satisfy his wife's craving. The next day she was craving banana, also a forbidden food and soon after she wanted some goatfish to eat, yet another food forbidden to women. Leimakani sensed that his wife was pregnant which was why she was experiencing these cravings and believed that his ancestral gods were testing them with these desires.

Leimakani went to a prophet in his village to see if he was correct and when he arrived the prophet already knew why he was there and confirmed Leimakani's suspicions. The prophet explained that Hina was pregnant and that the cravings were the unborn child's cravings and not Hina's. He also told Leimakani that his son would do great deeds and outwit dangerous supernatural beings and punish any who brought misfortune upon the family. The prophet encouraged Leimakani to control his wife's cravings and told him not to worry his wife with stories of misfortune for this would harm her child in the womb.

Hina was delighted to hear that she was pregnant, for they never expected to have a child, especially at this late stage in their lives. She was pleased that now they would have someone to care for them in their old age. On the day of his birth, Leimakani was sure that the prophet had been right about the great things his son would accomplish for a terrible storm raged on land and sea when Hina was about to give birth. The child was thus named Punia, "the overwhelming of the land and sea."

Punia was a very strong child and very large for his age. He followed his father everywhere, to the garden and the ocean. They were constant companions and loved each other very much. Punia became a very good farmer and, like his father, he worked hard, unlike many children his age. Leimakani told Hina that if his death preceded hers that he would not worry for he knew Punia would take good care of them both. These words were a blessing for Hina to hear, although they did not think long about Leimakani's death, he had forgotten the prophet's warning of misfortune.

By the time Punia was seven his father decided he was ready to go to the lobster cave where he always went to get lobster for the family. Punia got a lobster easily but his father would not let him dive alone. When Punia was ten he was as strong as an eighteen year old and could beat all the older boys in his village at anything. Leimakani was an expert at physical activities and taught him how to spear, box, race and fight with a stick. Punia became so competent at these skills and was so strong that he often hurt the other children and even adults in the village when they would have a fighting contest.

During this time, a very large shark and his army of ten other sharks came into the home sea of Leimakani, where they began to kill and eat the swimmers and divers of the area. Leimakani had not heard about these sharks and the damage they were inflicting on his village people and went to dive for lobster at his usual cave with Punia. Punia wanted to dive with his father, but for some reason Leimakani insisted on diving alone. The shark chief, Kai'ale'ale ("tumultuous sea"), overheard their conversation and was very disappointed for he had hoped to have a meal of two humans instead of just one for himself and his army. Kai'ale'ale waited for Leimakani to dive into the cave and get his lobster then attacked him as he was beginning to surface. Leimakani was torn apart and devoured by the sharks, and the shark chief raised his head above the water to show Punia what he had done to his father. Punia's grief was overwhelming and with tears of sadness and rage in his eyes he raised his fist to Kai'ale'ale and vowed to avenge his father's death.

By the time Punia reached home, he was wailing and pounding his chest with grief and his mother could hear him approach. As soon as she saw him in his sorrowful state she knew that her husband had somehow been harmed. She asked Punia why he was crying and where his father was. Punia told her of Leimakani's terrible death, how he was torn apart by the shark chief and his warriors. Hina wept bitterly at the news and wanted desperately to join her husband in the sea but her love for her son deterred her.

Punia and Hina mourned the death of Leimakani. Punia comforted his mother but secretly committed himself to avenging his father's death. He kept busy in his father's garden, but his mother forbid him to go diving for lobster. He was obedient during the time of mourning for he didn't want to disturb his grieving mother, but when the mourning time was over he told her how much he had been craving seafood and asked her if he could go to the cave for some lobster. His mother became very upset but he insisted promising her that he would just go with his fishing pole and not diving. When he returned they enjoyed a dinner of sweet potato and fish which they hadn't had in a long time.

After several days, Punia was again craving seafood and again he requested permission from his mother to dive for lobster in his father's cave. She refused his request, but he was so insistent that she finally begged him to be very careful and not dive if it wasn't safe. Punia went down to the ledge overlooking the cave and saw the shark chief and his band of sharks lying there. He spoke in a loud voice, knowing Kai'ale'ale would hear, about his plans to dive down and get lobster for his dinner. Kai'ale'ale quickly woke up his warriors and warned them to be alert. Punia announced his readiness to dive then threw a rock far from the cave which fooled the sharks into swimming in that direction. As soon as they had left the cave area he quickly dove and was standing on the ledge with two lobster in hand laughing at the sharks when they returned. He then told Kai'ale'ale that the shark with the skinny tail had told him how to escape from the jaws of the rest. The shark chief quickly found the shark with the skinny tail, killed him and let the rest of the sharks devour him.

Hina was overjoyed to see Punia and his catch of lobsters and quickly made a fire to roast them. Punia was happy that a sacrificial companion of one of the sharks had joined his father and he planned his next attack on the shark chief and his army. His mother again tried to keep him from diving for lobster but finally realized that his mind was made up; he was committed to his plan to destroy the sharks who had destroyed his father. Punia repeated the same trick on the sharks, throwing a rock to the other side of the cave which the sharks chased while Punia dove and quickly caught lobster for his mother and himself. Again he blamed the trick on another shark, again Kai'ale'ale killed that shark and the others devoured him. Punia continued with his plan until the only shark remaining was the shark chief.

Punia asked his mother to prepare a finely woven mat and he cut two sticks and also got rubbing sticks for fire making. He gathered kindling, salt, a shell scraper and a small knife and put all of these supplies in a woven bag. He told his mother that he would be gone for about twenty days, kissed her and left for the lobster cave. He announced loudly that he was going to dive down and hoped that if Kai'ale'ale caught him that he would not swallow him whole for if he did he would surely die, but if he tore him apart then Punia's mother would be able to use the blood on the surface to bring him back to life. Taking his supplies with him he leaped into the open jaws of the gigantic shark who easily swallowed him whole. Just as the great shark was about to close his mouth, Punia propped it open with the two sticks and stuffed the tightly woven mat into the space to keep the saltwater out. He then made a fire, scraped some meat of the shark off the inside of his belly, roasted it and ate.

The shark finally came ashore in Kona and the villagers, seeing the huge shark, decided to kill it. The villagers began beating Kai'ale'ale and he thrashed about hoping to kill Punia inside of him but they beat him more. Before they finally killed the shark, Punia told Kai'ale'ale, "My plan to avenge my father's death is now complete and just as you ate my father's body so will the people of Kona eat you. After the shark's death the people began to cut him up with sharp knives and stone adzes. Punia cried out from inside, "Be careful or you'll cut up the man inside." One man heard the voice in spite of the loud chatter of the crowd and told the other's to listen, after making fun of the man for hearing things, they too heard the voice and were afraid that the shark was haunted and ran away.

Another group of people arrived and began to cut up the shark and again Punia cried out from inside. They also were frightened and ran away. The first group returned with a crowd that joined them as Punia was trying to devise a plan to get out of the shark. He feared that the people would be angered for scaring them off if he just came out of the shark. He remembered his bald head which he knew was unique and put it inside a hole which he made in the mat so the mat became a cape. He waited until twilight and emerged from the mouth of the shark while shouting loudly. The people were terrified as they saw the shiny head and ash colored face wearing a cape run towards them. They all ran away in fright and never turned to look back at the monstrous sight of the clever son of Hina and Leimakani chasing them.

West Indian

The Faithful Friend

Once upon a time, on the island of Martinique, there lived a wealthy man. Unfortunately, this gentleman's beloved wife had died giving birth to their only son, Clement, and so the gentleman hired a widow from a nearby town to care for his child. Now the French-born widow had a son of her own named Hippolyte.

The two boys grew up like brothers and loved each other dearly. They enjoyed the same games and books. They both grew to be tall and handsome, Clement with skin the deep color of cocoa, and Hippolyte with fair skin only lightly tanned by the tropical sun.

One day, Clement showed his friend a small painting of a young woman. "This is Pauline. She is Monsieur Zabocat's niece. I am in love with her. I am going to journey to her home in Macouba in order to ask her uncle for her hand in marriage. Will you come with me, dear friend?" asked Clement of Hippolyte.

Now, Hippolyte had heard tales of Monsieur Zabocat who was thought to be a wizard of sorts. He knew that there was a good deal of mystery surrounding Monsieur Zabocat and that Clement's journey might prove dangerous. Yet, he could see the happiness in his friend's face when he spoke of Pauline. He did not want to disappoint Clement by mentioning Monsieur Zabocat's wizardry so he agreed to go. "As long as my dear friend is happy," thought Hippolyte, "then I am happy," and they set off for Macouba the next day.

The sun was blazing in the brilliant blue sky and the men were excited to be on their journey. All around them were the fragrant blossoms and luscious fruit of the island. Their adventure had begun happily. But just as they approached Macouba, they discovered a beggar sick and suffering in the heat along the side of the path. "We cannot leave that poor man this way," said Hippolyte. "Let us carry him into the shade of the banana grove and give him something to drink."

The two young men lifted the weakened man into the grove and placed him in the cool shade of a tree. There they gave him food and drink and stayed until they were sure of his comfort. Although it was much later in the day when they set off again, they were happy to have been of help.

Finally, at twilight, they reached Monsieur Zabocat's large estate. Clement was flushed with excitement, yet Hippolyte remained wary. At last they met the master of the House. "Good evening, sir," said Clement as he introduced himself and his good friend. Hippolyte noticed the warm glances cast between Clement and Pauline, as well as the cool stare of Pauline's uncle, Monsieur Zabocat.

After the young men spoke of their journey, Monsieur Zabocat invited them to stay for dinner out of respect for Clement's father, although his manner remained cold. Servants set the table with fine china and silver and the meal which followed was exquisite. There was spicy soup, and fresh crab, there were rich sweets and luscious fruit. At the end of the meal, Clement could wait no longer to declare his love for Pauline. He knelt before her and asked her to marry him.

When she accepted, her uncle grew furious. "I forbid it!" he declared. "I shall decide when and whom you shall marry and that is that!"

But Pauline was just as devoted to Clement as he was to her. "Dear uncle," she began, "I am so grateful for all you have done for me. But I am old enough to know my heart and I will marry Clement."

This outraged Monsieur Zabocat. In anger he swept the fine dishes from the table. "Then get out! None of you are welcome any longer!" The three young people rose to leave. Monsieur Zabocat raised his finger toward them, "But take care," he said in a low voice, "you are not married yet! We shall see if your marriage is to be." His eyes were fierce and the young people fled quickly so as not to anger him any more.

The moon was high in the night sky as they left Monsieur Zabocat's mansion. Pauline could not help weeping over her uncle's cruel words. Clement could not bear to see his beloved so unhappy. "Do not be sad. We are together and my father will welcome you with open arms when we arrive home. I am certain he will make peace with your uncle."

Clement's words soothed Pauline, and as they walked into the night, the three talked and laughed until they became weary and stopped to sleep beneath some trees. But Hippolyte was troubled by an unnatural silence around them until all at once he heard the beating of drums in the dark distance. While his friends slept he ventured into the forest. The sound of the drums led him to a clearing where he came upon three beautiful women. Hippolyte hid as he listened to the first woman say,"The lovely young girl and the handsome young man are asleep." The second woman nodded,"Yes, it is time for us to do what the great wizard Zabocat called us to do!" With that, the third woman cried out, "The spell must begin!"

Hippolyte was trembling as he realized that no matter how beautiful they were, these must be evil spirits summoned by Monsieur Zabocat to keep Pauline and Clement from getting married. He hoped they would not discover him as he continued to listen.

"Tomorrow, early in the morning, the couple will arrive at a stream," said the first woman.

"They will be so very thirsty and will drink from it," said the second.

"And then they shall die," confirmed the last. Then she added in a low voice, "If anyone should repeat this plan, his legs will turn to stone."

The women vanished into the darkness, and Hippolyte crept back to watch over his friends.

When morning finally arrived, the others awoke and Hippolyte urged them to continue the journey quickly. He knew he could say nothing of what he had heard the night before. Before long, they did indeed come upon a stream. "Oh, let us have a drink," said Pauline, "before we go on our way." Hippolyte scooped up the murky water, saying, "This water is not at all suitable for drinking. I fear it would make you very ill." In spite of their thirst, they walked on.

In the heat of midday, they paused to rest. While Pauline and Clement cooled themselves beneath the shade of a tree, Hippolyte scouted the area for any sign of the wicked ladies. He spotted them nearby in a grove of mango trees. "This time we shall not fail," said the first lady as she passed a ripe mango to the second one. "They will soon come upon this grove," cackled the second as she handed the fragrant fruit to the third lady. "Yes!" cried the third, "And they will eat the fruit and die!" She glanced around and added, "If anyone should tell of this plan, he will turn to stone up to his chest."

Once again, the women vanished and Hippolyte returned stealthily to his friends. When he found them, they were eager to start off on their journey. After only a few moments, they came upon the mango grove. Pauline was so anxious to eat the fruit but Hippolyte stopped her. He picked one and pretended to take a bite and spit it out. "It's terrible!" he said, grimacing. "Surely, these mangoes are poisonous!" he cried as he tossed the fruit away. Sadly, Pauline turned away from the trees and the three continued on.

As the day grew hotter, the friends stopped on the roadside to cool themselves. Ever vigilant, Hippolyte wandered restlessly near the forest. Once again, he came upon the evil women.

"We shall not be foiled this time," murmured the first of the ladies. "Once the young couple enters the house, they shall die."

"Ah yes," agreed the second,"on their wedding night they shall be stung by a serpent."

"And if anyone tells of this plan, he shall turn to stone from head to toe!" cried the third as she pulled a writhing serpent from her pocket, just before the three of them disappeared once again.

Hippolyte slipped off to rejoin his friends and hasten them on their way.

At long last, the trio arrived at the home of Monsieur Duforce. Happy to see the group, Monsieur Duforce welcomed them warmly and expressed his great joy over his son's engagement to the lovely Pauline. He assured them that he would set things right very soon with her uncle.

A few days later Monsieur Zabocat did, in fact arrive, saying that he would attend the wedding and that he had forgiven the couple. But Hippolyte, after all he had witnessed on their journey remained suspicious. In spite of Monsieur Zabocat's smiles and pleasant manner, Hippolyte sensed a viciousness which was terrifying. He watched and waited for the horrible serpent to appear but it did not.

The day of the wedding arrived. The couple looked more glorious than ever, Clement in a fine dark suit, and Pauline in a flowing white satin gown. Friends gathered excitedly at the home eager to celebrate the happiness of the young couple. As guests flocked to the garden to toast the bride and groom, Hippolyte hurriedly sharpened his cutlass inside, preparing to protect his dear friends against the worst. As soon as the couple entered the house, the huge deadly serpent appeared as if from nowhere. Writhing quickly toward the couple it raised its head to attack. At that very moment, Hippolyte lunged at the creature, striking it with his sharpened cutlass, and to everyone's shock the horrible serpent vanished into thin air.

People had gathered to witness the terrifying event and from amongst them Monsieur Zabocat cried out,"Hippolyte is jealous of his friend's happiness. He brandishes the sword with which he tried to harm the newlyweds!" Hippolyte knew he could not reveal what he had learned in the forest lest he turn to stone, so he had no choice but to gaze sadly at his friends. Stunned, Pauline and Clement did not know what to make of their dear friend's silence. "You have nothing to say for yourself, do you?" Monsieur Zabocat continued loudly. "You could not bear their happiness, so you were going to strike them both down with your cutlass!"

Hippolyte could no longer stand to see the sadness and confusion in the eyes of his treasured friends. He began to tell of his first encounter with the wicked women. As he spoke, his legs turned to stone.

"Stop! You need tell us no more," pleaded Clement. But Hippolyte wanted his friend to know the whole truth, and continued to tell him about the deadly mangoes. Immediately, his body hardened up to his chest.

"Please, dear Hippolyte, say no more!" implored Pauline. But Hippolyte was driven out of faithfulness to his friends. As he finished his story, he turned completely to stone from head to toe.

At that moment, an old man moved forward from the crowd.

"I can bring him back to life on one condition," spoke the old man softly.

"Anything," said Clement eagerly, "I will do anything."

"You must take this curse upon yourself. Only then can I release your friend," the old man explained.

"I shall do it gladly. For he has saved my life many times over," said Clement as he embraced his new bride.

"Very well," said the old man, and he waved his hand before the stone face of Hippolyte, then blew gently over him.

At once, Hippolyte came to life again, but before he could say a word, the old man moved to touch Clement with the tip of his finger. Monsieur Zabocat leaned forward, eager to see the young man he detested turn to stone. Suddenly, the old man turned in the direction of none other than Monsieur Zabocat and touched him with his outstretched finger. It was Monsieur Zabocat who was turned to stone!

The old man looked kindly at Clement. "The spell was broken by your eagerness to give your own life for your friend's. The kindness you show to others returns to you." He smiled, and in the next instant disappeared.

Clement and Hippolyte turned to look at one another in amazement. "Was that not the same poor man we helped along the roadside at the beginning of our journey?" asked Clement. Hippolyte shook his head. "Surely it couldn't be," he replied. "Or could it?" he wondered again. The two friends shrugged, smiled warmly at each other, and embraced.

In the time that followed, Clement and Pauline lived very happily, and Hippolyte fell in love and married as well. The friends remained true and dear to each other always.

As for the statue of Monsieur Zabocat, it was placed in a corner of the garden, where it quickly turned to dust.

PROVERBS AND MAXIMS

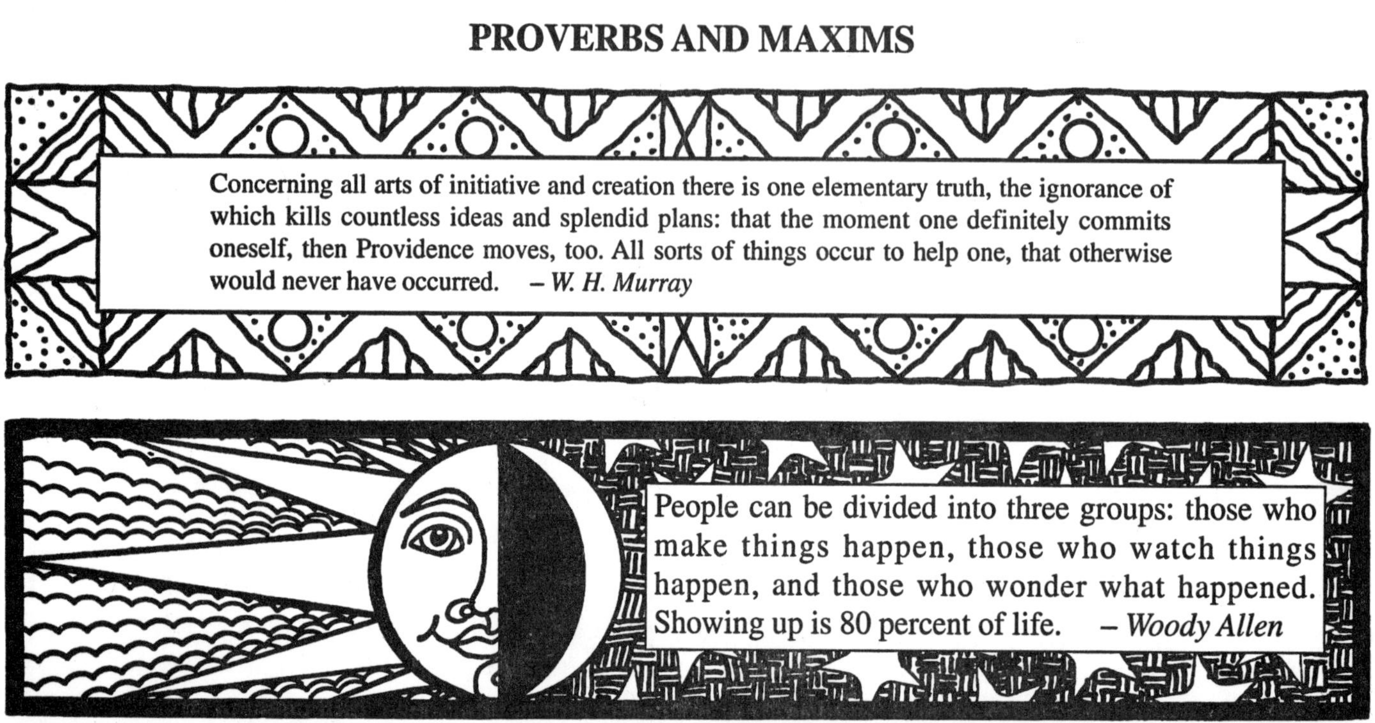

Concerning all arts of initiative and creation there is one elementary truth, the ignorance of which kills countless ideas and splendid plans: that the moment one definitely commits oneself, then Providence moves, too. All sorts of things occur to help one, that otherwise would never have occurred. *– W. H. Murray*

People can be divided into three groups: those who make things happen, those who watch things happen, and those who wonder what happened. Showing up is 80 percent of life. *– Woody Allen*

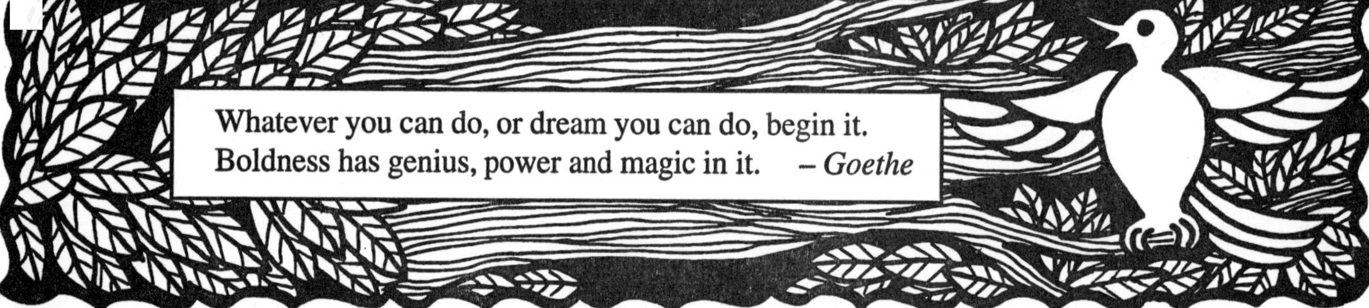

Whatever you can do, or dream you can do, begin it. Boldness has genius, power and magic in it. *– Goethe*

The important thing in life is to try to be your best. Be honest with yourself and make an honest commitment to yourself, your family, your friends, and your community. An honest commitment means 100 percent. It means self-discipline, it means loyalty, and it means being able to be counted on in the clutch. *– Joe Paterno, College Football Coach*

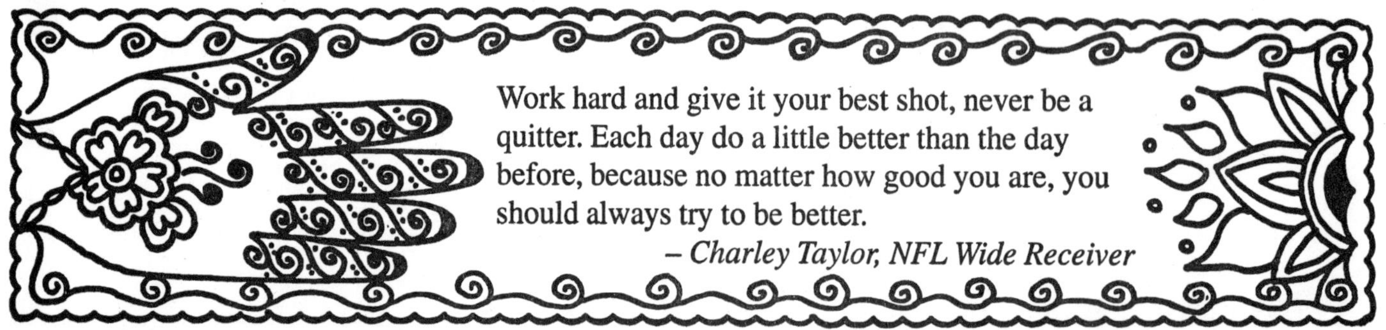

Work hard and give it your best shot, never be a quitter. Each day do a little better than the day before, because no matter how good you are, you should always try to be better.

– Charley Taylor, NFL Wide Receiver

HEROES AND HEROINES

EARL E. BAKKEN (1924–)

Born in Minneapolis, Minnesota, he was educated in the Columbia Heights public schools and the University of Minnesota with a degree in electrical engineering. Earl was always fascinated with electricity; while he was a teenager, he made a robot that could smoke cigarettes. At age nine, when he saw the original *Frankenstein* movie, he decided he wanted to make electrical instruments that could help people. He co-founded Medtronic, Inc. in 1949 and in 1957 developed the first wearable, external, battery-powered, transistorized pacemaker. This pacemaker has developed through several revisions and is used by millions of people. His medical devices have transformed and saved millions of lives. Retiring in Waimea, Hawaii, he heads the Board of Directors of the North Hawaii Community Hospital. Already recognized as a center for healing, it emphasizes a balance of technology and medical innovations with the human touch and spirituality. His work embodies a lifetime commitment to human service and healing.

DIANE FOSSEY (1932–1985)

Born in San Francisco, California, she graduated from San Jose State College in 1954 with a degree in occupational therapy. She worked for several years in a children's hospital in Kentucky; then, in 1963, inspired by the writing of American zoologist George B. Schaller, she traveled to Africa. She visited the British anthropologist Louis Leakey and observed mountain gorillas. These encounters changed her life completely, and she stayed in Africa. She became an astute and patient observer of gorilla behavior, knew each as an individual, and regarded them as gentle social animals. She established the Karisoke Research Center in 1967, which became an international center for gorilla research. She spent twenty-two years studying the ecology and behavior of the mountain gorilla, and her book *Gorillas in the Mist* (1983) recounts much of this research. In 1985 she was found murdered at her campsite; some authorities believe she was killed because of her efforts to stop the poaching of gorillas. As a result of her research and conservation efforts, the mountain gorillas are protected by the government of Rwanda and by the international conservation and scientific communities.

VINCE LOMBARDI (1913–1970)

Born in Brooklyn, New York as the first of five children of an Italian immigrant, Vince was raised in a strict Catholic environment. He studied for the priesthood for two years, but changed his mind and his school. He majored in business at Fordham University and starred on the football team as a guard, where he was a member of the famous "Seven Blocks of Granite." In 1939, while studying law in night school, he took a job as a high school teacher and assistant football coach. He quickly moved from this small beginning to Fordham and then to West Point, where he developed his basic coaching philosophy. He was hired by the New York Giants as an offensive coach and earned the reputation of a coach who could take a poorly performing team and produce a winner. In 1958 he became head coach of the Green Bay Packers, where his philosophy and success became legendary.

PUT COMMITMENT INTO ACTION

- Do something today that you promised to do yesterday.
- Thank a member of your family for doing a good job with one of their responsibilities.
- Work a little harder or a few minutes longer on a duty or assignment that is difficult for you.
- Choose a job you've been putting off, decide to commit yourself to the job until it's done, and then do it.
- Recognize a friend or teacher who has fulfilled their responsibilities—tell them or write a note to them.
- Put some extra effort into something that is difficult and try to improve your skill.

COMMUNITY SERVICE IDEAS

- Commit to an ongoing project with Ronald McDonald House (or other community outreach program). Volunteer to take them toys and books, make holiday decorations, go for visits, and sing to them.
- Make signs to hang up around your community telling people about the value of commitment.
- Encourage community commitment to a goal of reducing the amount of energy used each month. Remind them of the many ways to do this (for example, turn off the lights of an unoccupied room and turn off the water while brushing your teeth).
- Plan for a family night at home. Be sure everyone understands the significance of committing to this time to be together.

BOOKS ON COMMITMENT

Harald and the Great Stag. Donald Carrick. New York: Clarion Books, 1988.

King's Fountain. Lloyd Alexander. New York: Dutton, 1971.

Many Lives of Chio and Goro. Betty Jean Lifton. New York: W. W. Norton, 1968.

Moss Gown. William Hooks. New York: Clarion Books, 1987.

Sir Gawain and the Loathly Lady. Selina Hastings. New York: Lothrop, Lee & Shepard Books, 1985.

The Book of Virtues. William J. Bennett, ed. New York: Simon and Schuster, 1993.

"The Ants and the Grasshopper " – p. 354
"The Commercial Artist" – p. 140
"The Farmer and His Sons" – p. 370
"Hercules and the Wagoner" – p. 359
"The Little Red Hen" – p. 352
"Paul Revere's Ride" – p. 708
"Penelope's Web" – p. 701
"The Sheep and the Pig Who Built a House" – p. 356
"The Song of the Bee" – p. 349
"The Thousandth Men" – p. 736
"The Three Little Pigs" – p. 357
"Tom Sawyer Gives Up the Brush" – p. 398

SUPPORTIVE VALUES **Friendship • Sincerity**

DEFINITIONS **Unselfish kindly concern for the good of another.**

Love is probably the most written about subject in the world. The question of what love really is has always been a mystery. M. Scott Peck writes, "Love is too large, too deep ever to be truly understood or measured or limited within the framework of words." Henry Drummond refers to love as the summum bonum—the supreme good. Drummond points out that in a letter to the Corinthians, Paul wrote, "Now abide Faith, Hope, Love, these three; but the greatest of these is Love." Paul also wrote, "Love is the fulfilling of the law." It is the highest of rules, Drummond contends: "It is the rule for fulfilling all rules, the new commandment for keeping all the old commandments . . . " Much has been written about the kinds of love which can be felt: filial or brotherly love, erotic or romantic love, and agape, which is an interest in and care for the welfare of another. Agape is the kind of love to which we are referring as the value for this month.

Friendship fits our above definition of love and the **sincerity** with which we express our feelings for each other is important. Too often we express our friendly feelings in insincere ways. Sincerity connotes honesty and challenges us all to be more honest in our dealings with people.

PURPOSE Sarcasm is a common mode of expression and regardless of how witty we think we may be, the real risk of hurting another remains. Sarcasm is the antithesis of sincerity. It is, as Ambrose Bierce remarked, " . . . the questionable weapon of questionable intellects." Again our emphasis on respect and The Golden Rule in our first month is a logical explanation for being more cautious of our use of sarcasm in class. Affirmation and encouragement would better exemplify how we can care for others in more sincere, friendly, and loving ways.

Love — February

Day One: Discuss the meaning of love using the definitions on page 103.	**Day Two:** Work with a partner to practice pronouncing love in different languages. (See page 105.)	**Day Three:** In small groups, use the discussion questions on page 106 to guide your thinking and learning about love.	**Day Four:** How does receiving love feel? Draw a picture to represent that feeling. Select colors and textures to use which best represent your feelings!	**Day Five:** Why is it sometimes difficult to love a particular person? Why is it important to love even those you find hard to love? Share your ideas with a classmate.
Day Six: Discuss with your class whether animals feel love for each other or for humans. Share an experience that justifies your position.	**Day Seven:** For show and tell, share with your classmates someone or something you love.	**Day Eight:** In a total class setting, read and discuss one of the stories about love on pages 107-112.	**Day Nine:** Remembering yesterday's story about love—write your own short story about love OR write the lesson on love that yesterdays story taught you.	**Day Ten:** Choose, color, and cut out one of the bookmarks on page 113. Keep it in one of your books to remind yourself to be loving each and every day.
Day Eleven: Prepare to celebrate Valentine's day by selecting (out of a hat containing classmates' names) a secret Valentine.	**Day Twelve:** Make an original Valentine's Day card for your secret Valentine.	**Day Thirteen:** Celebrate Valentine's Day by giving the card you made to your secret Valentine.	**Day Fourteen:** Find your soul mate to discuss the true meaning of love with. Some people believe that a soul mate is someone who shares the same same "heart" as another. Cut paper hearts in half in a random zigzag pattern, so that no two are alike. Students must match their half with their "soul mate"!	**Day Fifteen:** Brainstorm with your class ways to show love with friends, with family, with neighbors. (This is a good time to talk about boundaries!)
Day Sixteen: As a class, choose one of the activities on page 116 and put love into action!	**Day Seventeen:** Divide the class into five small groups and assign a hero from pages 114-115 to each group. Then provide time for groups to draw a picture of their hero putting love into action.	**Day Eighteen:** Select a community service idea from page 116. Plan to make it happen.	**Day Nineteen:** Follow through on your community service plan you made yesterday.	**Day Twenty:** Reflect on what you have learned this month about love. Think about how you can embrace love throughout your life.

LOVE IN OTHER LANGUAGES

Chinese	*ai*	to love; to be fond of; to like; love and affection
French	*l'amour*	interior movement of devotion directed towards God, an ideal, another person; very strong emotion or attachment involving tenderness and physical attraction between two people
German	*liebe*	love, affection, kindness, passion, charity
Hawaiian	*aloha*	love, affection
Japanese	*ai*	a merciful mind that gives people food
Korean	*sa rang*	amour
Latin	*amor*	from Old Norse "lofa" (to love); related to Latin "libere" (to be pleasing) (something pleasing)
Spanish	*amor*	love, affection
Tagalog	*pagmamahal*	a fond, deep, tender feeling toward someone

DISCUSSION QUESTIONS

- How can we show love in our classroom? Outside of our classroom? At home?
- Why is it important to try to be a loving person?
- What are some examples of love we see everyday in the classroom? On our campus? At home?
- What are the expressions of love that you appreciate receiving?
- Why is it important for everyone to receive love?
- How do people become friends?
- What is most important in being a good friend?
- Can you have more than one friend? How many can you have?
- Can family members be friends?
- How do you know if someone means what they say? If they'll keep a promise? Why is this important?
- How would you define love? (not romantic love)
- What are some of the ways this love is expressed between good friends?
- Is it possible to share this kind of love with someone you don't know?
- What's the difference between concern for a friend and concern for someone who is homeless?
- What are the qualities you look for in a good friendship?
- Do your friends look for those qualities in you?
- How long does it take to build a good friendship?
- What can harm a friendship? Can those things be overcome and the friendship be rebuilt?
- How important is sincerity in a relationship? Why?

STORIES AND THOUGHTS FROM SPIRITUAL TRADITIONS

Hinduism

Love expects no reward. Love knows no fear. Love Divine gives—does not demand. Love thinks no evil; imputes no motive. To love is to share and serve.

– Swami Sivananda

One would incur great sin even seeing those who are not distressed at the suffering of a friend.

– Ramcaritmanas

View your own Everest-like pain as nothing more than a grain of dust, while to minuscule problems of a friend as being like a mountain.

– Ramcaritmanas

Buddhism

Love is wishing happiness for living beings. Boundless love is wishing ultimate happiness for infinite living beings, without expecting anything in return.

Hatred is not overcome through hatred, but through love alone.

Love for All

One day the Buddha came upon a group of children who had caught a crab and begun to torture it. The children squealed as one boy ripped off the crab's claws and then its legs, one by one. The Buddha asked the children, "Would it hurt you if someone ripped off your legs?" "Yes," they replied. And the Buddha asked, "Doesn't the crab feel pain just like you? Not only does the crab suffer, but its family members also suffer when the crab feels pain. Think this over carefully." As the children reflected and began to regret their actions, the villagers gathered to hear the Buddha's teaching: "Every living being wants happiness and safety. All living creatures—large and small, two-legged and four-legged, swimmers or fliers—all have the right to live. Therefore, let us harm no living being. Let us protect life. Just as a mother protects her only child even at the risk of her own life, so should we, too, with open hearts, protect all living beings from harm. Day and night—whether sitting, standing, walking, or lying down—let us be full of love, surrounded by love on all sides. Let us dwell in love always."

Zen Buddhism

Isshin (one-heart) means to throw oneself wholly into the action without any other thought at all.

Christianity

"Let love be genuine; hold fast to what is good." – *Bible, Romans 12:9*

"So faith, hope, love abide, these three; but the greatest of these is love."
– *Bible, I Corinthians 13:13*

"And above all things, put on love, which binds everything together in perfect harmony."
– *Bible, Colossians 3:14*

"This is my commandment, that you love one another as I have loved you."
– *Bible, John 15:12*

Islam

By Him in whose hand my soul is, ye shall by no means enter paradise until ye believe, and ye shall by no means believe until ye love one another.

– Selections from Mishkat-ul-masabi [444] p 99
Abu-Hurayrah, MU: AB: TI

Shall I tell you of a thing which when ye do, ye will love one another? Extend greetings among yourselves.

– Selections from Mishkat-ul-masabi [445] p 99
Abu-Hurayah, MU

Allah's Messenger said: 'None of you has faith unless he loves for his brother what he loves for himself.'

The love of Allah and His Prophet Muhammad necessarily leads to the love of His Creation. When we have truly cast our gaze from material rewards and turned to Him, then our hearts will turn naturally to love of our fellow man. Love of this kind is not simply a matter of treating another as we would have him treat us, but of genuine empathy which goes beyond concern for our own lot.

– The Essential Teachings of Islam p 3
4: Hadith (Bukhari) 2:6

Chinese

"Is Goodness indeed so far away? If we really wanted Goodness, we should find that it was at our very side."

– Confucius

"One who has accumulated moral power will certainly also possess eloquence; but he who has eloquence does not necessarily possess moral power."

– Confucius

"When soul and body are in the bond of love, they can be kept together. By concentration on the breath it is brought to perfect elasticity, and one becomes as a babe."

– Lao Tzu

The flowery branch of the wild cherry
How swiftly it flies back!
It is not that I do not love you;
But your house is far away.

The Master said, "He did not really love her. Had he done so, he would not have worried about the distance."

– The Analects, Book IX

Jan Jung asked about Goodness. The Master said, "Behave when away from home as though you were in the presence of an important guest. Deal with the common people as though you were officiating at an important sacrifice. Do not do to others what you would not like yourself. Jan Jung said, this is a saying I shall put into practice.

– The Analects, Book XII

Judaism

More Love

Rabbi Pinhas and his disciples reflected on the advice of the Baal Shem in regard to dealing with difficult people. He said that when it is clear that someone dislikes you and wants to do you harm it is necessary to encourage your spirit to love them more. This is the only way that you can make a difference in the relationship. If love and unity prevail among people then the Divine Presence and holiness surrounds them. But if a chasm develops between people then the potential holiness falls into the chasm. So if your neighbor is distant from you in spirit you must bring yourself closer to him, to close up the gap between you.

Native American

The Love Flute

Once there was a young man who was deeply in love with a beautiful young girl, but he was so shy that he could not bring himself to tell her how he felt. In fact, it was easier for him to go into battle against fearsome enemies than to face the girl he loved. He was brave enough to lead in the buffalo hunt, but he did not have the courage to tell the girl how much he loved her.

Now, there were other young men who were drawn to the beautiful maiden, as well. They waited proud and confident outside her tipi until she emerged, ready to offer her their lovely blankets and to speak to her. The shy young man looked on from a distance, becoming more and more disappointed in himself. He thought about her every minute of the day and she even filled his dreams at night. Still, he could say nothing.

Each day the beautiful maiden would go to the river to fetch water and the shy young man would stay to watch her. The other young men gathered, too, whistling or throwing pebbles to attract her attention. She would smile at them as she passed. It seemed so easy for them to talk and laugh with her. "I think she likes us!" one proud young man said to his friends one day.

"She must like them a lot," thought the shy young man, "after all, they speak to her so easily. They manage to say whatever they want. They chat with her each day. She doesn't even notice me."

His love for her remained quiet, but strong. Yet, the young man grew sadder and sadder with each passing day. He cared little about anything as life for him without the beautiful girl was so empty. One morning, he set out away from the camp, moving aimlessly up the mountainside. Out of sadness and frustration, he shot an arrow high into the sky without aim.

To his surprise, the arrow did not arc downward, but continued to fly far and high in the sky. The young man followed it and managed to keep pace with it throughout the entire day. Finally, at dusk, the arrow curved earthward and fell next to a clear stream. The next morning, the young man sent another arrow flying. He followed it throughout the day until it once again landed near a clear stream. He did the same for four days, sensing that unseen powers were helping him and leading him to something wonderful.

On the fourth evening, he found himself at the edge of a wood. He was tired after his pursuit of the arrow and he lay down to rest. He could not say whether what happened next was real or a dream. He heard the leaves rustling nearby, and the sound of voices whispering around him. "You tell him," said the first. "No, you," a second voice replied. At that moment, two large Elk Men with towering antlers emerged and stood over him.

One bent toward the shy young man, saying, "Here is something for you." He held a beautiful flute which next he put to his lips and played. "You see how lovely its music is? It is made of cedar which grows where winds blow. The woodpecker made these holes for playing. All the other birds and animals helped to make it as well, and we have put our voices inside it. When you play it, you will hear our voices in your songs. The music you make with it will sing to the heart of the girl you love. It will tell her of your love."

Suddenly, there was a flash from a mirror carried by one of the Elk Men, and the young man was blinded. As he tried to regain his eyesight, he saw two bull elks running into the trees. He picked up the flute which had been left behind, and holding it he felt as if something had changed. He blew into the flute and birds all around him joined in his song.

For four days, he made his way back to the camp. He played the flute as he walked and made music with the songs of the birds and sounds of the animals. His songs carried throughout the forest and gave pleasure to all the creatures there.

On the fourth evening, he entered the camp playing his lovely flute. The light breeze carried his songs through the camp and straight to the heart of the beautiful girl he loved so dearly. She knew his music was meant for her. It called to her and she left her tipi to find the young man. When she came upon him, she sat down close to him and listened to the music of his flute. It told her more than words could ever say. "I love you" it sang, over and over.

PROVERBS AND MAXIMS

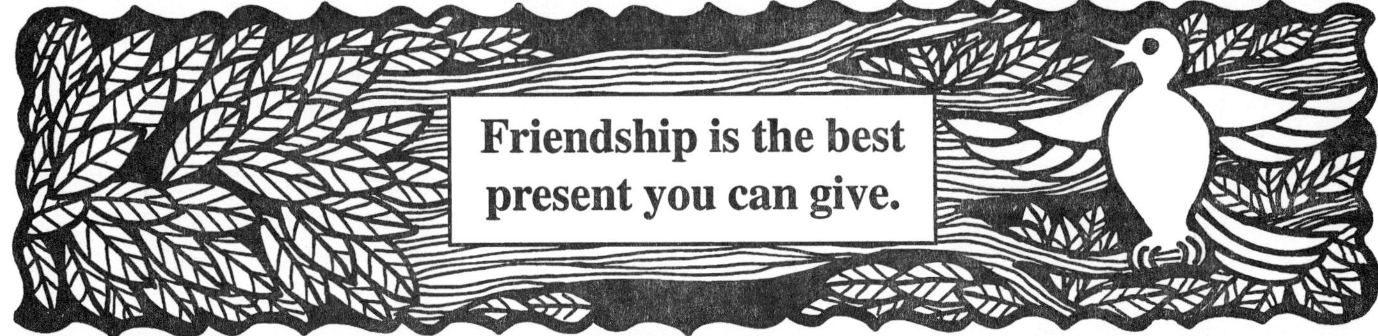

It is good to love many things, for therein lies the true strength, and whosoever loves much, performs much, and can accomplish much, and what is done in love is well done. – *Vincent Van Gogh*

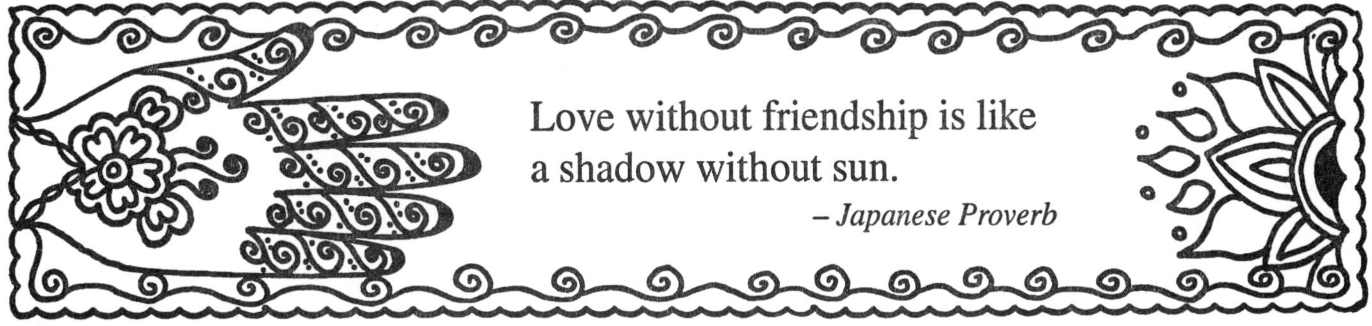

HEROES AND HEROINES

THOMAS ANTHONY DOOLEY (1927–1961)

Born in St. Louis, Missouri, he developed an early interest in serving people and chose medicine as the best way to accomplish his goals. He joined the Navy in 1953 and within a year was involved in providing medical relief for Vietnamese refugees. He established a medical mission in northern Laos in 1956, followed by hospitals in Cambodia and Vietnam. In 1957 he established Medico, an international medical aid mission. He wrote several books that reflect on the needs of people and the connections between morality and the human spirit: *Deliver Us from Evil, Edge of Tomorrow* and *The Night They Burned the Mountain.* He is an excellent example of the many physicians who chose a service of love over a lucrative medical practice. His early death cut short a promising life of commitment to the world's health needs.

ELIZABETH FRY (1780–1845)

She was born in Norwich, England into a family that had belonged to the Society of Friends (Quakers) for generations. Her father, John Gurney, was a successful banker. When Elizabeth was seventeen, she became a Plain Quaker, dressing in plain clothes and giving up all personal adornments. She married a London merchant named Joseph Fry, also a Quaker. In 1813 she learned about the terrible conditions in Newgate Prison. Located in one of the oldest and worst parts of London, it housed over 400 women and 50 children in four small rooms with no beds, no heat, no toilets, no ventilation and no light. She visited the prison, encouraged the women, and started talking to prison officials and lawmakers about improving the conditions. Because the behavior of the prisoners improved when they were treated better, her ideas spread throughout England. Soon rulers from France, Denmark, Holland and Prussia asked for her advice. Her actions of love and kindness reformed the prisons and the laws of much of Europe.

ANNE MANSFIELD SULLIVAN MACY (1866–1936)

Born in Feeding Hills, Massachusetts, near Springfield, Anne was the teacher who became the lifelong friend of Helen Keller. Anne married John Macy in 1905. In 1887, at age 21, she was chosen as the teacher of Helen Keller, who was without sight and hearing and unable to speak. Where others had failed, Anne Sullivan didn't give up, and with as much love as skill and teaching techniques, taught Helen to speak. Her patient and courageous love enabled the frightened and underdeveloped Helen to become a mature and successful person. In time, they were close friends and companions.

JOHN MUIR (1838–1914)

Born in Dunbar, Scotland, of rather harsh and pious parents, he moved to America with his family in 1849. They settled near Portage, Wisconsin. Forbidden to waste daylight hours on reading, John was granted permission to get up early. So, he invented a machine that would dump him out of bed at one o'clock in the morning. He studied science and medicine at the University of Wisconsin but gave it up for jobs that challenged his inventive skills. In 1867, he changed his mind again, giving up his own inventions "to study the inventions of God." He began walking across America, keeping a journal of scientific and personal observations as well as pencil sketches. His writings as a naturalist and an explorer are still important to conservationists. His love of nature and his exploration of Yosemite Valley were instrumental in establishing Yosemite National Park.

ST. FRANCIS OF ASSISI (1182–1226)

Born in Assisi, Italy, and given the name Giovanni, he was called Francis by his father, a successful cloth merchant who raised him to appreciate luxury. When he was twenty, Francis was taken a prisoner of war and underwent several religious experiences. As a result, he renounced any claim to his father's wealth or name and entered a life of poverty and service to others. He thought the church needed to return to the original message of Christ, which was to love all people and all creatures. A number of young men were inspired by his example and asked to join his way of life. In 1209, they presented their ideas for a new religious community to the Pope, and the order of Franciscans was formed. By 1223, he was spending more and more time in prayer and meditation, leaving the decisions about the order to others. His last two years were spent in constant pain and near blindness. He was canonized as a saint two years after his death.

JANE GOODALL (1934–)

Born in London, England she moved with parents and sister to Bournemouth on the English coast. While she did well in her studies, Jane much preferred learning about animals and insects, and playing outside. The love of all creatures began when she was two years old after her mother gave her a stuffed toy chimpanzee. Once, she was caught sleeping with earthworms under her pillow and, another time, waited for five hours for a hen to lay an egg. Unhappy with life as a secretary, she left for Nairobi, Africa in search of the famed paleontologist Louis F. B. Leakey. She won Leakey's trust and admiration. The scientific world was amazed when Leakey sent this twenty-four year old woman, who had worked only as a waitress and a secretary, into the wilds to study chimpanzees. Her ability to observe, to collect and analyze scientific data, and write reports as an animal activist earned her worldwide acclaim as an ethologist. Her love for animals is seen in this statement about the chimpanzees: "Surely we must speak for them—for they cannot speak for themselves."

PUT LOVE INTO ACTION

- Continue practicing The Golden Rule.
- Invite someone who is all alone to play with you.
- Make a new friend.
- Compliment someone on something.
- Tell your parents and other family members that you love them.
- Offer a word of encouragement to someone who is struggling with some work.
- Speak with someone you don't know very well.
- Say what you mean nicely, without sarcasm.
- Continue with your random acts of kindness.

COMMUNITY SERVICE IDEAS

- Plan and carry out a "Love in a Baggie" project by filling a gallon bag with toiletry items and a happy message, to be delivered to a shelter for the homeless.
- Help make "Goody Sacks" by filling paper bags with small toys to be delivered to kids in the hospital.
- Send Valentines to adults in a local senior center.
- Create "love your neighbor" signs to hang up in public buildings within your community.
- Collect paper back books to be placed in waiting rooms at social service centers.
- Make special "love notes" for members of your family.

BOOKS ON LOVE

Girl Who Loved Wild Horses. Paul Goble. Scarsdale: Bradbury Press, 1978.
A Mother for Choco. Keiko Kasza. New York: Putnam, 1992.
Porcelain Man. Richard Kennedy. Boston: Little, Brown, 1976.
The Stupids Have A Ball. Harry Allard. Boston: Houghton Mifflin, 1978.
Wolf's Chicken Stew. Keiko Kasza. New York: Putnam, 1987.

The Book of Virtues. William J. Bennett, ed. New York: Simon and Schuster, 1993.
"How Robin Hood Met Little John" – p. 308
"Rocking Horse Land" – p. 286
"The Selfish Giant" – p. 292
"The Velveteen Rabbit " – p. 275

A Call to Character. Collin Greer and Herbert Kohl, eds. New York: Harper Collins Publishers, 1995.
"The Little Prince" – p. 429
"The Magic Locket" – p. 415
"More Adventures of the Great Brain" – p. 420

SUPPORTIVE VALUES **Knowledge • Insight**

DEFINITIONS **Deep understanding; the ability to choose and act with sound judgment.**

Wisdom is a trait we admire as we age, and a quality we acquire as we become more aware of our surroundings, our relationships, and ourselves. Often we think it is a characteristic obtained through experience, yet educators all know of the wisdom read in students' work or observed in their interactions with each other, regardless of their age and despite their seeming lack of experience and knowledge.

Knowledge and **insight** are used in defining wisdom, and ideally education is a vehicle for obtaining wisdom. Through the experiences which we offer our students academically, socially, musically, artistically, physically, and spiritually–knowledge and insight are natural results. Yet we are cautioned by the wise, "You must not hold a thought just because many other people hold it, nor because it has been believed for centuries, nor because it is written in some book which men think sacred; you must think of the matter for yourself, and judge for yourself whether it is reasonable." (J. Krishnamurti) This is essentially the process of critical thinking which we prize so highly and strive to develop in our students. Gibran says it another way, that the wise educator "does not bid you enter the house of his wisdom, but rather leads you to the threshold of your own mind."

PURPOSE The purpose of highlighting wisdom as a value which we honor is twofold. We acknowledge wisdom as a virtue which we recognize in others and strive to obtain for ourselves, so that we may better serve others. "Study then, but study first that which will most help you to help others. Work patiently at your studies, not that men may think you wise, not even that you may have the happiness of being wise, but because only the wise man can be wisely helpful." (J. Krishnamurti) We are all capable of making wise decisions when we take the time to look at the various choices and the consequences of those choices. Much of what we refer to as wisdom is an awareness of what is happening in and around us. If we develop awareness we are taking our first steps toward wisdom. In becoming knowledgeable and understanding, we can make wiser choices regarding our relationships and our actions as they affect the world around us.

Wisdom — March

Day One: Discuss the meaning of wisdom. Does wisdom also mean intelligence? Is there more than one type of wisdom?	**Day Two:** Think of all the people you know personally who impress you as being very wise. Name one "wise person" of your acquaintance. Beside that person's name write one or two sentences explaining what caused you to include them on the list.	**Day Three:** Do you think modern technology is helping people of today gain wisdom or could it possibly encourage people to be less concerned with seeking wisdom? Explain your answer.	**Day Four:** Write or draw a journal entry about an act or a decision on the part of one of your teachers or school administrators that you feel demonstrated wisdom.	**Day Five:** Write a creative story. Tell of one person's search for wisdom.
Day Six: Why and how should we respect the wisdom of others? How does the wisdom of adults benefit kids' 1) health 2) education 3) safety?	**Day Seven:** Imagine what a world without wisdom would be like. Discuss your ideas with your classmates. Would you like to live in such a world? Why or why not?	**Day Eight:** One way to gain wisdom is by learning to communicate with other people. Name and give examples of ways students in your class are gaining reading, writing, speaking and listening skills.	**Day Nine:** Increase your wisdom by pronouncing together the word wisdom in different languages on page 121.	**Day Ten:** Proverbs and maxims often seek to impart wisdom. Make a bookmark from the proverbs on page 137. Discuss with your classmates the wisdom contained in the proverb you have chosen.
Day Eleven: Read the stories about wisdom on pages 123-131. Why are stories a good way to share wisdom?	**Day Twelve:** Create a "Wise Student of the Week" award to be awarded to a student who demonstrated wisdom in his or her actions and decisions that week.	**Day Thirteen:** Select a student to receive the "Wise Student" award and describe the actions that caused you to select that person to receive the award.	**Day Fourteen:** Remember a time when you shared some of your wisdom with another person. Write or draw about the experience in your journal.	**Day Fifteen:** Do some research in the library to find a mythical figure which represents wisdom. Some ideas are: unicorns, magicians, wizards, and dragons. Remember to also look into Greek and Roman mythologies! Draw a picture of this character. Display for the whole class to view.
Day Sixteen: How do you think the saying, "the wise old owl" came into being? Why do you think the owl became a symbol of wisdom? What other animal might become a symbol of wisdom? Why? What traits might cause a person to be labeled "wise"?	**Day Seventeen:** Write a thank you message to a person whose wisdom you often rely on to help you make decisions or solve problems.	**Day Eighteen:** Does a person necessarily have to be educated to be wise? How are wisdom, education, and intelligence alike and different?	**Day Nineteen:** Encourage wisdom at home by checking out a book on wisdom from your library and taking it home to read tonight with your family. (see list on page 137 for book suggestions)	**Day Twenty:** People of your age can begin now to gain wisdom for the future. Reflect on the importance of developing respect for wisdom as a desirable value at an early age and on ways young people can begin to establish goals and habits that lead to wisdom.

WISDOM IN OTHER LANGUAGES

Chinese	*zhi*	wisdom; knowledge; cleverness; prudence
French	*la sagesse*	characteristic of a person showing itself in right judgement, aware and informed decisions and actions; also, behavior of obedient, tranquil child
German	*weisheit*	to have wisdom, knowledge, learning
Hawaiian	*na'auao*	learned, enlightened, intelligent, wise
Japanese	*chi*	the God entered into a person and one keeps talking
Korean	*hyun myung*	wise and bright; acumen; discernment
Latin	*sapientia*	from Gothic "-witi" (wit) (having one's wits together)
Spanish	*sabidura*	wisdom, knowledge, learning
Tagalog	*karunungan*	being wise in conduct and words; knowledge and good judgement based on experiences

DISCUSSION QUESTIONS

- Why is it so important that everyone be given the opportunity of going to school?
- What are people supposed to learn in school?
- What do you enjoy learning? How do you think it will help you?
- What is an example of something that is hard to understand? Why is it hard? What could help you understand?
- How would you explain the purpose of school to someone your age who has never had the opportunity of going to school? Would they like to go to school or feel sorry for you?
- What are the most important things you are supposed to learn in school?
- What would you like to learn?
- What are the ways knowledge will help you as you grow older?
- How does knowledge increase your appreciation and understanding of other people? Other cultures?
- Are there important things that you learn outside the classroom? Without books?

STORIES AND THOUGHTS FROM SPIRITUAL TRADITIONS

Hinduism

He who knows little speaks much.
He is wise who speaks little, but his words have great value.

– *Tradition*

The person who possesses the innocence of childhood, vigor of youth, and wisdom of old age is capable of truly knowing the Divine.

– *Tradition*

In the land of the blind, the one-eyed is king.

– *Tradition*

Christianity

Solomon the Wise King

The Lord appeared to King Solomon in a dream one night and told him to ask for anything he wanted, and it would be given to him!

Solomon replied, "You were wonderfully kind to my father, David, because he was honest and true and faithful to you, and obeyed your commands. And you have continued your kindness to him by giving him a son to succeed him. O Lord my God, now you have made me the king instead of my father, but I am as a little child who doesn't know his way around. And here I am among your chosen people, a nation so great that there are almost too many people to count! Give me an understanding mind so that I can govern your people well and know the difference between what is right and what is wrong. For who by himself is able to carry such a heavy responsibility?"

The Lord was pleased with his reply and was glad that Solomon had asked for wisdom. So he replied, "Because you have asked for wisdom in governing my people, and haven't asked for a long life or riches for yourself, or the defeat of your enemies—yes, I will give you what you have asked for! I will give you a wiser mind than anyone else has ever had or ever will have! And I will also give you what you didn't ask for—riches and honor! And no one in all the world will be as rich and famous as you for the rest of your life! And I will give you a long life if you follow me and obey my laws as your father David did.

Then Solomon woke up and realized it had been a dream. He went to Jerusalem and went into the Tabernacle. And as he stood before the Ark of the Covenant of the Lord, he sacrificed burnt offerings and peace offerings. Then he invited all of his officials to a great banquet.

Soon afterwards two young prostitutes came to King Solomon to have an argument settled.

"Sir," one of them began, "we live in the same house, just the two of us, and recently, I had a baby. When it was three days old, this woman's baby was born too. But her baby died during the night when she rolled over on it in her sleep and smothered it. Then she got up in the night and took my son from beside me while I was asleep, and laid her dead child in my arms and took mine to sleep beside her. And in the morning when I tried to feed my baby it was dead! But when it became light outside, I saw that it wasn't my son at all."

Then the other woman interrupted, "It certainly was her son, and the living child is mine."

"No," the first woman said, "the dead one is yours and the living one is mine." And so they argued back and forth before the king.

Then King Solomon said, "Let's get the facts straight: both of you claim the living child, and each says that the dead child belongs to the other. All right, bring me a sword." So a sword was brought to the king. Then he said, "Divide the living child in two and give half to each of these women!"

Then the woman who really was the mother of the child, and who loved him very much, cried out, "Oh, no, sir! Give her the child—don't kill him!"

But the other woman said, "All right, it will be neither yours nor mine; divide it between us!"

Then the king said, "Give the baby to the woman who wants him to live, for she is the mother!"

Word of King Solomon's decision spread quickly throughout the entire nation, and all the people were awed as they realized the great wisdom God had given him.

– Bible, 1 Kings 3:5-28

Islam

Just as the unfolding of the Qur'an to the Apostle and his people was a gradual process, so it is for any individual who approaches it. True knowledge can never be grasped all at once by anyone other than Allah. So we must be patient, allowing the meaning and purpose of the Qur'an to unveil itself according to our own capacity and Allah's Will. We must be humble in the realization that our knowledge can never be complete; there is no end to what we can learn from it, the complete Revelation and final Revelation of Allah.

– The Essential Teachings of Islam p 148
231: Mystic Letters TH (TA HA) 20:114

Chinese

"To learn and at due times to repeat what one has learnt, is that not after all a pleasure? That friends should come to one from afar, is this not after all delightful? To remain unsoured even though one's merits are unrecognized by others, is that not after all what is expected of a gentleman?"

– Confucius

"He who learns but does not think, is lost. He who thinks but does not learn is in great danger.

– Confucius

Chen and the Great Bronze Bell

Long, long ago in China there lived a very wise man named Chen. He was not only clever, but he was also fair, and was admired and respected by all. People who sought justice would come to Chen, seeking his advice and accepting his decisions.

One night there was a great robbery committed in the district in which Chen lived. The people were outraged and angry. Several suspects were rounded up quickly, but no one could be certain as to who the thief really was. All of them were questioned for hours and still the townspeople could not decide who the guilty one was. It was decided that they all should be taken to Chen. Certainly he would be able to solve the mystery.

Chen listened to each person's story, but instead of asking them questions he simply said,"There is a great bronze bell which hangs in the temple to the East. It will be able to tell us who the robber is."

Chen sent several men to carry the beautifully polished bell from the temple to the town, for it was extremely large and heavy. When the men finally arrived with it, Chen ordered them to construct a cloth canopy over it. They made it from a large square of cotton which they mounted on four poles. Once they were done, Chen sent the men away. He set firepots to burn all around the great bell. The fires burned through the night and when they finally died away, Chen carefully removed the poles and let the cotton canopy fall gently so that it completely covered the great bell like a blanket.

The next day people from all around came to see the bell and to witness the trial. They knew that Chen would identify the thief and they wanted to see how he would do it. There were so many people that there was scarcely any room for the suspects. When everyone was assembled, Chen stood before them and said, "This old bronze bell has powers beyond my own. It can determine guilt and innocence with speed and certainty. Ten thousand innocent people may rub it and it will not make a sound. But should one thief touch it, the bell will sound for people to hear for miles around!" Then Chen knelt before the bell and made a prayer over it. He turned to the suspects and said, "Each one of you shall reach under the cloth and rub the bell. It will sound when the guilty one touches it."

One by one, each suspect approached the bell and slipped one hand under the cloth to rub it. As each one turned away from the bell without having made it ring, the crown let out a sigh. When the last one had passed the test and no sound was heard the crowd became restless. The bell had failed! But Chen moved forward and clasped the arm of the last suspect. "Here is our thief!" Chen exclaimed.

The accused man turned to the crowd and said, "That's ridiculous! The bell made no sound when I touched it. I am as innocent as all the others."

It was then that Chen instructed some men to remove the cover from the bell. People could see that the once shiny bronze bell was now blackened with soot. There were shiny streaks where the suspects' hands had rubbed the soot away.

"This bell has truly great powers." declared Chen. "Indeed, it made no sound when innocent people rubbed it. Neither did it ring when the thief put his hand under the cover. But alas, the thief was afraid to touch it lest he make the bell sound out his guilt. Thus, only the hands of the thief remain clean and free of soot." All eyes fell to the blackened hands of the innocent suspects, then to the clean hands of the guilty man.

All agreed that Chen possessed great power and wisdom indeed.

Hawaii

The Owl Who Saved the Boy

Na'ilima was playing a string game while waiting for her brother to finish fishing in the bay below her. She watched a school of silvery fish come near him and wondered if he saw them. He threw his net at the right moment and pulled the catch in. She was proud of her brother who was a skilled fisherman even though he was just a young boy.

While she was watching her brother, she didn't see a canoe enter the bay. The men paddled toward the beach where her brother was pulling in his catch. They took away his net and threw the fish back into the ocean. They surrounded him, tied him up, and put him into the canoe and paddled away. Na'ilima was so worried about her brother she began to cry. Why have they taken my brother? He must have broken a kapu since one of the men was a priest. He could die if he broke a kapu. She followed the canoe along a cliff trail overlooking the sea and saw that they took her brother to a temple. They were going to kill her young brother!

She started praying to her family guardian god, the owl. "Please save my brother. He did not know that he was breaking a kapu . . . please save him." She repeated her prayer over and over. Soon an owl appeared and perched near Na'ilima as if to say he had heard her prayer and was going to help. He flew off toward the temple.

At dusk the owl perched on a wall of the temple and saw that the guards were asleep. He flew over and with his powerful beak he began to pull on the cords that bound the boy. The boy's hands were now free, so he could untie his feet. Once freed he quietly climbed the temple wall, although he was aching and sore. He started to run toward the path that would take him to his sister, but the owl struck him with his strong wings. The boy understood that the owl didn't want him to run and didn't want him to face the direction he wanted to go. As frustrated as he was the boy understood that for some reason he was being forced to walk backward by the owl, whom he knew to be his guardian, so he obeyed. Whenever he tried to turn and run the owl would strike him with his wings until he turned backward and walked.

Finally they came to the rock where Na'ilima sat praying and crying with worry. She quickly embraced her brother then heard voices in the distance coming toward them. "It must be those who captured you," she whispered. "Hide in this hole under the rock." The men with torches arrived and asked her if she had seen anyone. "No one has come this way," she replied.

"Here are his tracks!" yelled one of the guards. "He went this way!" exclaimed another who held his torch over a footprint in the soft dirt. They all hurried off, following the tracks that the boy had made back to the temple. The brother and sister ran quietly off together and were soon safe at home.

India

Something that is Everything

One day Emperor Akar was galloping back to Agra when he saw a crowd under a banyan tree. He heard that a very wise sage sat there. Akbar returned to the place disguised as a commoner, met the sage, and asked him to pass on some wisdom.

"Give me something that is everything and I will give you wisdom," said the sage.

Akbar was puzzled. Back in the palace Akbar told his friend Birbal what puzzled him. "My lord, I have plenty of that thing!" said Birbal. Both Akbar and Birbal, disguised, proceeded to meet the sage. Akbar was surprised that Birbal was not carrying anything with him.

"Have you brought something that is everything?" the sage asked Akbar. Akbar looked at Birbal. Birbal picked up a handful of dust. "Here it is. Man or monument, prince or pauper, sage or fool, plant or animal, all become dust. This is something that is everything," said Birbal.

The sage looked at Akbar and said, "You wanted wisdom from me. One who has this man as his friend needs no wisdom from me."

Japanese

The Wise Old Woman

Long ago, in a village in the hills of Japan, there lived an old woman and her son, a farmer. They lived a simple, but good life. But the village was ruled by a cruel young lord who imposed many strict laws over the villagers. One day he issued a proclamation. "Anyone over seventy years of age is no longer useful to the village," were the lord's harsh words. "Any person who reaches that age is to be taken into the mountains and left to die."

When the young farmer's mother reached her seventieth birthday he was saddened by what he had to do according to the lord's rule. He could not bear to take his mother far from their home and leave her alone to die. His heart broke with the thought of carrying out the lord's command. But his mother knew of his duty. Placing her hand gently on that of her son, she said, "The time has come for you to take me into the mountains."

So, sadly, the next morning, the son carried his beloved mother on his back along the steep mountain path. The trees grew dense and the air chilly as he made his way higher and higher. The mother snapped twigs from the trees and dropped them as he walked, saying, "I am marking the path for your safe return, my son."

The son could bear the heartbreak no longer. "I will not leave you alone in the mountains, mother," he said. "I am taking you back to our home and I will never leave you."

With that, protected by the shadows of the night, he carried his mother all the way back down the mountain path to their home. He dug a secret room beneath the kitchen where his mother spent her days. She was so well hidden that no one knew of their secret.

A few years had passed when one day there was a great commotion as some of the great Lord Higa's warriors descended on the village in a whirlwind. They rode up to the young lord's estate and shouted for him to hear. "This is a warning from the mighty Lord Higa," they cried. "In three days time he will sweep through your village and conquer it!"

The young lord was cowardly and implored of them, "Please spare my life. I will do anything you ask!"

"Lord Higa has no pity for you or your little village," one of the warriors replied. "He does, however, have great respect for a clever mind. If you solve the three impossible tasks written on this scroll, you and your village will be spared."

The young lord caught the scroll as the warriors turned and thundered off. Nervously, he unrolled the scroll to reveal the first impossible task. "The first task is to make a coil of rope out of ashes," it read. "Secondly," the young lord continued to read, "you must run a thread all the way through a crooked log. And thirdly, you must make a drum that plays without being hit."

The young lord quickly called the very wisest people of the village to his palace. He commanded them to solve the impossible tasks, but try as they might they could not come up with the solutions. They begged the gods for help, but there was no response.

In a panic, they sought the cunning badger who lived in the forest and who had outsmarted people many a time. "Please, help us!" they implored. But even the badger was not clever enough to solve the impossible tasks.

The young lord was furious when the wisest people of the village returned to him without answers. "You are nothing but fools!" he cried, and swiftly threw them into prison. He was now desperate to find the answers and offered a bag of gold to anyone who could help him. The news of the lord's plight and the threat to the village spread quickly.

The young farmer spoke to his mother of the impossible tasks. "This is terrible," he said. "In no time at all our village will be conquered by yet another cruel lord."

His mother remained silent for a few moments as she thought. Then she told her son to bring her a coil of rope, a crooked log, and a small drum. When he returned with the objects, she began by soaking the coil of rope in salt water, then leaving it to dry completely. Then, she lit one end of it with a match. They watched as the flame traveled through the rope all the way to the other end. The young farmer was amazed that although the burning rope had turned to blackened ashes, it did not crumble, but instead, held its shape. "There is your rope of ash," she said.

Next, she picked up the gnarled and crooked log. She dabbed a bit of honey on one end of it, and at the other she placed an ant to which she had tied a silk thread. The ant, eager to find the honey, made its way through the twists and turns of the log, all the while pulling the silk thread. When it finally arrived at the honey the mother said, "The second task is done."

Lastly, she took the small drum and opened up the skin on one side. She placed a bumblebee inside and resealed the drum. The bee flew about within the drum, trying to escape. It hit against the skin repeatedly, making the drum play without being beaten. "And now the last task has been completed," the mother said calmly.

The young farmer ran to his lord's palace and presented the solutions to him. The lord was amazed and could not believe that the farmer had been clever enough to complete the tasks. "Surely someone must have helped you. Who is it that had the wisdom to do this?" the lord asked sternly.

The farmer confessed that in fact, it was his wise old mother who had solved the problems. He admitted that he had kept her hidden for several years as he could not bear to leave her in the mountains on her seventieth birthday. "She is the one who has saved us from the threat of Lord Higa," the farmer said. He waited for the lord to unleash his fury for disobeying the law.

But the young lord sat quietly, looking at the poor farmer. Finally, in a low voice he said, "I have been wrong. Our old people are of great value to us. I should never have sent them into the mountains to die, and it will be done no longer. From now on, they shall be treated with respect, and their wisdom will be treasured."

The next day, the young farmer marched with the lord's warriors to Lord Higa's castle. Upon their arrival, he presented the rope of ash, the threaded log, and the drum that played without being beaten to the mighty Lord Higa. A slow smile spread across Lord Higa's face. "So," he said thoughtfully, "you have solved the three impossible tasks. There must be much wisdom in your little village." Looking at the young farmer he said, "Go back to your lord and tell him that your people deserve to live in peace."

Never again was the young lord cruel or unfair to his people. The young farmer and his mother lived happily for the rest of their long lives.

PROVERBS AND MAXIMS

He who knows others is learned, he who knows himself is wise. *– Lao Tzu*

I never met a man so ignorant that I couldn't learn something from him. *– Galileo*

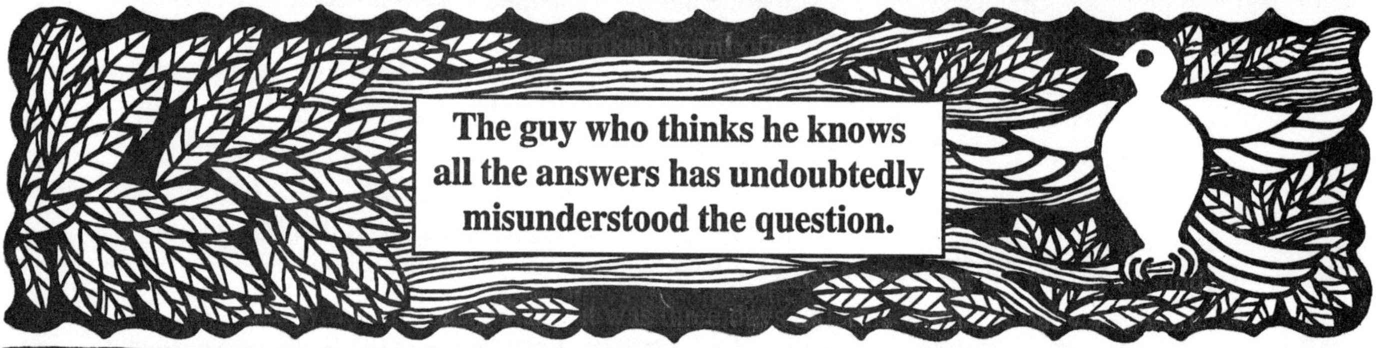

The guy who thinks he knows all the answers has undoubtedly misunderstood the question.

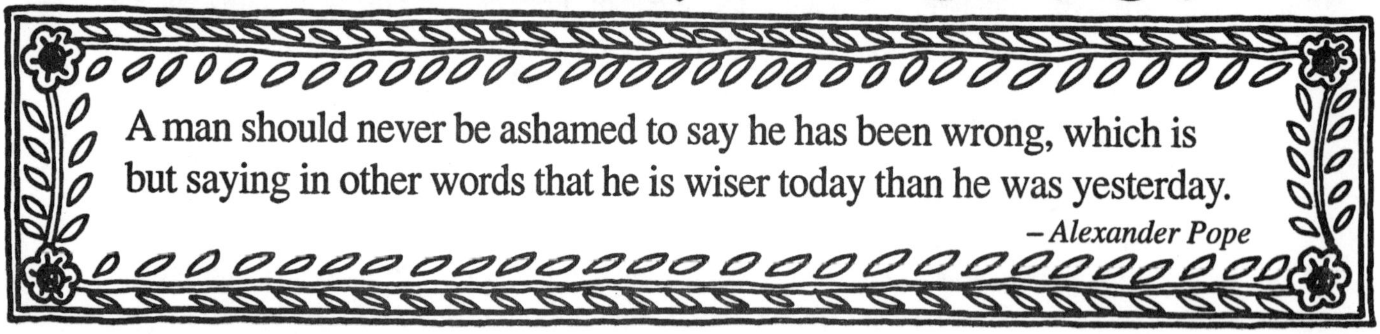

A man should never be ashamed to say he has been wrong, which is but saying in other words that he is wiser today than he was yesterday.
– Alexander Pope

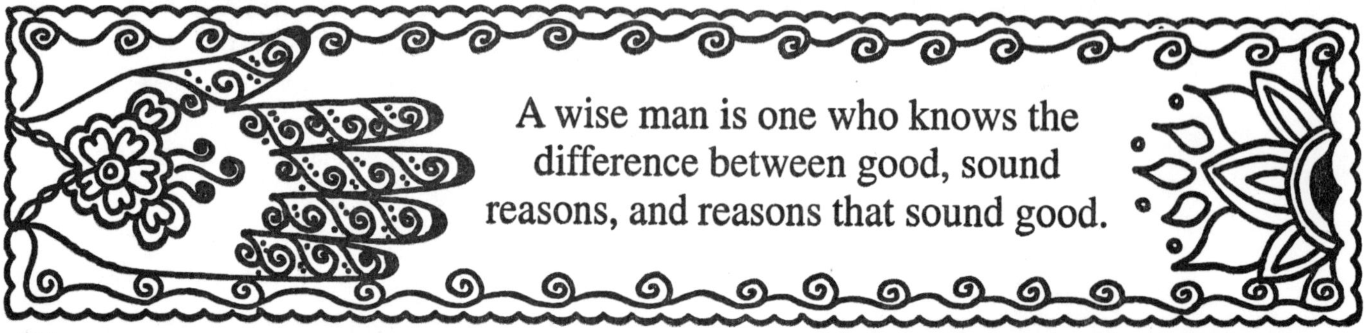

A wise man is one who knows the difference between good, sound reasons, and reasons that sound good.

HEROES AND HEROINES

DOROTHY DAY (1897–1980)

Born in Brooklyn, New York, she was the daughter of a newspaper sports writer who traveled widely with his family. Living in San Francisco and Chicago and never feeling close to family or friends, Dorothy developed a love for literature and writing. College life and a core of radical friends gave her a foundation of new social, cultural, and political ideas. Bored with college life, she moved to New York City and joined the Bohemian culture of Greenwich Village. World War I brought an end to this life, and she worked for a short time as a nurse. She drifted for several years as a writer and after the birth of a daughter immersed herself in religious literature and theology. She was baptized into the Roman Catholic Church and was faithful to the Church for the rest of her life. In 1932, she discovered a connection between her concern for justice and her religious faith and, with Peter Maurin, founded a newspaper that would communicate their views—the Catholic Worker. For the next fifty years she was a voice of wisdom for Catholic reform, the labor movement, the civil rights movement, the peace movement, and "liberation theology."

ALBERT EINSTEIN (1879–1955)

Born in Ulm, Germany, he grew up in and obtained his early education in Munich. Not exactly a child prodigy, he still wasn't speaking fluently at age nine. However, by age twelve he discovered Euclidean geometry and by age sixteen had mastered differential and integral calculus. He found school intolerable and was expelled because of his negative attitude. He failed entrance examinations to the Federal Institute of Technology in Zurich because of his lack of knowledge in other than scientific disciplines. There are only a handful of people who share the honor of initiating a revolution in scientific thought: Copernicus, Newton and Einstein are three. His insights into the natural world forever changed the world view of physicists and philosophers, and his achievements literally revolutionized physics. He is best known for his theory of relativity.

PLATO (428–347 B.C.E.)

Born in Athens, Greece of aristocratic parents, he lived his whole life in Athens. Little is known of his early years, but we know that he eventually traveled to Sicily, southern Italy and perhaps to Egypt. He was given the finest education Athens could offer, and he was a close associate of Socrates. When Socrates was unjustly executed, Plato turned in disgust from Athenian politics and focused his attention on philosophy. He founded the famous Academy, one of the great philosophical schools of antiquity, that existed for nearly a thousand years and had an enormous impact on the development of Western philosophy. Some scholars have suggested that the Academy may have been a type of religious brotherhood. His philosophical system attracted many followers in the centuries after his death and some of his ideas emerged in the movement of Neoplatonism that became a rival of early Christianity.

SOCRATES (469–399 B.C.E.)

Born in Athens, Greece, the son of a stone mason and sculptor, he learned his father's trade and practiced it for several years before turning to intellectual interests. He was also involved in three military campaigns for Athens. Though he was rather short in stature, he earned a reputation for great prowess and endurance in battle. There are accounts of his entering a kind of trance while in deep thought and he was observed offering prayers to the sunrise. Thus, he was an interesting mixture of warrior for justice, religious mystic, impromptu speaker, and teacher of philosophy and logic; his Socratic method of argumentation became famous. He was brought to trial on trumped-up charges of impiety and corrupting the youth of Athens, and he was forced to take the poison hemlock. Without founding a specific philosophical system, school, sect, or organization, and though he didn't profess any wisdom, his influence on people and on philosophy is immeasurable.

SOLOMON (ca. 980–925 B.C.E.)

Born in Jerusalem, he was the youngest son of David and Bathsheba. He inherited a huge kingdom and ruled with immense power and splendor. Both history and legend have attributed to him great wisdom. He became famous as a wise and fair judge and he is credited with writing three books of the Old Testament—Proverbs, Ecclesiastes and the Song of Solomon. He also possessed good diplomatic skills and was able to build important liaisons with other rulers. His forty-year reign was one of peace. He was responsible for the fortification of several towns in his kingdom and the construction of a series of elaborate structures in Jerusalem, including luxurious palaces, a wall around the city, and a magnificent temple on Mount Moriah. He sponsored industrial enterprises, built a great fleet of ships, and carried on extensive trade with other nations. To have "the wisdom of Solomon" has been the goal of many people.

PUT WISDOM INTO ACTION

- Discuss with your parents the wisdom of a particular character in a movie or video you've seen.
- Take some time to wonder about yourself, people, the world around you.
- Write about your wondering.
- Read a good book every week.
- Ask at least one good question every day.
- Talk with someone who is older than you about something you want to better know and understand.
- Be in the process of reading a good book all the time.
- Find someone you admire and question them about things they know about.
- Put extra time into a subject you have difficulty understanding.
- Decorate your classroom with symbols of wisdom. Draw an owl, a library, a college, a teacher, etc.
- Share some of the wisdom you learned today with your family. Then ask them to share some wisdom of their own!

COMMUNITY SERVICE IDEAS

- Become Pen Pals with residents of a retirement home; exchange ideas and learn from their wisdom.
- Collect books for a local literacy program.
- Volunteer to read to children in the hospital.
- Help collect school supplies for homeless children.
- Volunteer as a guide at a local museum.
- Research symbols of wisdom. Make banners or signs decorated with these symbols to remind members of your community of the importance of wisdom.
- Organize a read-a-thon. Ask for pledges from family and friends and select students and teachers to read in twenty minute slots. Keep it going for an entire school day! Donate the money to your school library for the purchase of books.
- Invite a grandparent of one of your classmates to share his or her wisdom about leading a fulfilled life.

BOOKS ON WISDOM

Fortune-tellers. Lloyd Alexander. New York: Dutton Children's Books, 1992.

Helga's Dowry: a troll love story. Tomi de Paola. New York: Harcourt, Brace Jovanovich, 1977.

It Could be Worse: a Yiddish folk tale. Margo Zemach. New York: Farrar, Struass, & Giroux, 1976.

A Penny a Look: an old love story. Harve Zemach. New York: Farrar, Strauss, & Giroux, 1971.

Wretched Stone. Chris Van Allsburg. Boston: Houghton Mifflin, 1991.

The Book of Virtues. William J. Bennett, ed. New York: Simon and Schuster, 1993.
"The Boy and the Nuts" – p. 46
"Boy Wanted" – p. 78
"The Frogs and the Well" – p. 52

Chicken Soup for the Soul. Jack Canfield and Mark Victor Hansen. Deerfield Beach: Health Communications, Inc., 1995.
"Sachi" – p. 290

A 2nd Helping of Chicken Soup for the Soul. Jack Canfield and Mark Victor Hansen. Deerfield Beach: Health Communications, Inc., 1995.
"Wisdom" – p. 301

A 3rd Serving of Chicken Soup for the Soul. Jack Canfield and Mark Victor Hansen. Deerfield Beach: Health Communications, Inc., 1996.
"God's Jobs" – p. 314
"The Secret of Life" – p. 319
"The Wisdom of One Word" – p. 316

April

SUPPORTIVE VALUES **Holistic Living • Serenity**

DEFINITIONS **The condition of being sound in body, mind and spirit.**

With all of the recent research concerning the mind-body connection, we are slowly becoming aware of how much our mental health affects our physical and spiritual health, and vice versa. This is knowledge which Asians have applied for centuries, and the Greeks and Romans espoused as well. The entire movement in holistic health is based on this idea, that our mind-body-spirit are interconnected, interdependent, and not separate, individual entities.

The partner values of **holistic living** and **serenity** emphasize the need to fully understand the importance of living a complete or whole life balancing physical, mental, social-emotional, and spiritual needs. "Utter calm and unruffled repose" are the poetic phrases which define serenity—the hopeful result of a healthy life.

PURPOSE One goal of teachers is to encourage students to become "well-rounded." This requires a commitment to providing an environment where students develop morally and spiritually, intellectually and physically, creatively and with an appreciation for the arts and for cultural diversity. There also is a desire to instill within them a sense of social responsibility. Health is a necessary component in the achievement of these goals. All of the basics in physical health—eat right, sleep enough, exercise regularly—are a good place to start. This month we will focus on how to live holistically and with serenity in our fragmented, often stressful workaday worlds. Darwin remarked, "If I had my life to live over again, I would have made a rule to read some poetry and listen to some music at least once a week; for perhaps the parts of my brain now atrophied would have thus been kept active through use. The loss of these tastes is a loss of happiness, and may possibly be injurious to the intellect, and more probably to the moral character, by enfeebling the emotional part of our nature."

Health — April

Day One: Discuss the meaning of health using the definitions on page 139.	**Day Two:** Use the discussion questions on page 142 to learn about health.	**Day Three:** List the five food groups. With your class, make a list of foods that fall into each category.	**Day Four:** Do you know the benefits of exercise? Do some research and share one fact you found with your class.	**Day Five:** How many types of exercise can you think of? Make a list.
Day Six: From the list of exercises you made yesterday choose one to do together as a class and do it!	**Day Seven:** We know that drugs can be very harmful to your health and some can even kill you! Practice with a partner how to refuse to accept drugs when they are offered to you.	**Day Eight:** The homeless need help to be healthy. Organize a food drive for your school. Be sure to request that students donate healthy food from the five food groups. After a one week collection, give the food to a local shelter or food bank.	**Day Nine:** Discuss whether being happy is an element of good health. How can you maintain this all important component of good health?	**Day Ten:** Why is going to a doctor for regular check-ups important for good health? Ask the school nurse or a visiting nurse from the community to visit your classroom and share expertise on this.
Day Eleven: What makes plants healthy? Make a list of things that they need to grow.	**Day Twelve:** Using what you know from yesterday, do an experiment. Plant grass seed in four different pots. Give one plenty of good soil, water and sunlight, put another in total darkness, don't water one, and don't give the fourth pot any soil. Watch the plants all week.	**Day Thirteen:** Record what your plants look like today in a science log.	**Day Fourteen:** How do your plants look today? Record what you see.	**Day Fifteen:** Make a judgement on which plant looks the most healthy. The same happens to people. Those who get what they need to grow healthy and strong live and grow!
Day Sixteen: Choose and color a bookmark from page 146. Put your bookmark in your health textbook to remind you to practice good health every day.	**Day Seventeen:** Brainstorm with your classmates and make a list of all the things you couldn't do if you didn't have good health. Name some things you could do to improve your health habits.	**Day Eighteen:** Read one of the stories about health on pages 143-145.	**Day Nineteen:** Choose a hero or heroine from pages 147-148 to read about. How did that person's efforts enable you to be more healthy today.	**Day Twenty:** Reflect on what you have learned this month about health. Determine to become more healthy by embracing this important value.

HEALTH IN OTHER LANGUAGES

Chinese	*jian*	strong, robust, vigorous; to strengthen; to invigorate
	shen	body
French	*la santé*	condition of a person whose organism is working well. Equilibrium of the personality and control of intellectual capacity
German	*gesundheit*	soundness of health, wholesomeness, salubrity
Hawaiian	*olakino maika'i*	good state of health (ola means "life, health, well-being," kino means "body, person, individual" and maika'i means "goodness, righteousness")
Japanese	*shinshin*	a balance of "mind and body"
Korean	*kun kang*	sound and vigor, well-being
Latin	*valetudo*	from Gothic "hal" (whole) (health is "wholeness"; related to "wholesome")
Spanish	*salud*	health, well-being, welfare
Tagalog	*kalusugan*	being well or not sick; freedom from sickness

DISCUSSION QUESTIONS

- When your body is sick, are you happy or sad?
- Why do you think your feelings are affected by your physical health?
- When you're sad, is your body affected? How? Why is this?
- How do you become physically healthy? Mentally healthy? Spiritually healthy?
- What makes you feel better when you're physically sick? When you are unhappy? When you don't know why you feel bad?
- Why do people become sick when they are worried? When they're afraid? When they're bored?
- What other emotions affect you physically?
- What can a person do to keep the body, mind, and spirit healthy? Why?
- Is it difficult to maintain the proper balance? Why? What works for you? What part do you try to improve first? Why?
- Do you need other people to feel better or can you rely on yourself? Does faith help?

STORIES AND THOUGHTS FROM SPIRITUAL TRADITIONS

Hinduism

The key to realization and liberation is a healthy body.

– Charaka Samhita

A soft stomach [i.e., no gastric problems], warm feet [i.e., good circulation], and a cool head [i.e., no fever, anger, etc], lead to long life.

– Tradition

As you eat, so you think. – Tradition

Food that is prepared or given with love is filled with spiritual nutrition. Food that is not should not be eaten.

– Tradition

Buddhism

Buddha Shakyamuni taught that there are 84,000 different emotional afflictions—arising from desire, hatred, and ignorance—which affect beings adversely and produce 84,000 different physical disorders. Illness is common to all living beings, and ultimately the way to eliminate it is to purify the mind.

The Buddha is likened to a doctor, the spiritual teachings are like medicine that cures the afflictions, and spiritual friends are like the nurses who help administer the medicine.

Moderation is the key to physical well-being. Avoid eating too much, talking too much, or thinking too much. A healthy person is one who achieves physical and mental balance.

The physical, intellectual, and spiritual well-being of each person are integrally related. Curing the body alone, without paying attention to a person's mental and spiritual health, is insufficient. The human organism is a dynamic whole. When the humors of the body—wind, bile, and phlegm—are in balance, we enjoy health and happiness. When the humors get out of balance, we are vulnerable to various afflictions. A calm and positive state of mind is essential for maintaining optimum health. Ailments can also be treated on a karmic level, by creating good deeds such as saving lives, practicing generosity, reciting mantras, and practicing meditation. Imagining ourselves surrounded and filled with the light of compassion also helps prevent illness and injury.

Zen Buddhism

We often compare the state of our minds to that of our stomachs. When we are in good health, we forget that our stomachs even exist. But, as soon as we have a stomachache, we are continually conscious of the pain there. This is because we don't pay attention to our bodies until we become ill. Only then, for the first time, we become conscious of the part that is ailing. In the same way as long as we live in peace and good health, we are not even conscious of our own selves.

Christianity

"For we are the temple of the Living God."

– Bible, II Corinthians 6:16

"Pleasant words are like a honeycomb, sweetness to the soul and health to the body."

– Bible, Proverbs 16:24

Islam

Whoso wakes up in the morning in the full security of his heart, and his body free from harm, having also his day's food, it is as though the world, all of it, is driven to him.

– Selections from Mishkat-ul-masabi [127] p 32
'Ubaydu'llah b. Mihsan, TI

The Prophet said, 'O 'Abdu'llah! I have been told that thou dost fast (all) day and standest up to pray (all) night.' I said, 'Yes, O Prophet of God!' He said, 'Then do not do (like that). Keep fast and eat also, stand up (to pray at night), and sleep also; for verily there is a duty on thee to thy body, and verily there is a duty on thee to thy people, and verily there is a duty on thee to thy visitors; and nobody has kept fast who fasted always: (a fast of) three days in every month is (equal to) constant fasting; so fast three days in every month.'

– Selections from Mishkat-ul-masabi [219] p 51
Aishah, AB: RA.

Chinese

"He that is really Good can never be unhappy. He that is really wise can never be perplexed. He that is really brave is never afraid."

– Confucius

Judaism

The Immersion Bath

The Baal Shem was very devoted to completely immersing himself in rivers or streams or a large bath. He believed that this practice was more beneficial to the body than abusing it by fasting for long periods or by hurting the flesh in other ways. These abusive practices were often done by those who thought they would make one more holy. The Baal Shem said that these practices only served to weaken " . . . the strength you need for devotions and teaching, the bath of immersion heightens this strength."

PROVERBS AND MAXIMS

Health and cheerfulness mutually beget each other. – *Addison*

He who has health has hope and he who has hope has everything.
– *Arabian Proverb*

It is part of the cure to wish to be cured.
– *Seneca*

God made our bodies temples for our souls, and they should be kept strong and clean to be worthy of the deity that occupies them.
– *Kahlil Gibran*

A wise man should consider that health is the greatest of human blessings. – *Hippocrates*

HEROES AND HEROINES

THE MAYO BROTHERS—WILLIAM JAMES MAYO (1861–1939) AND CHARLES HORACE MAYO (1865–1939)

Born the sons of an English medical doctor, William was born in Le Sereur, Minnesota and Charles was born in Rochester, Minnesota. Will and Charlie grew up surrounded by medicine and during the early evolvement of surgery. In 1889, a year after they had both received their medical degrees, the three Mayo physicians opened St. Mary's Hospital. Their nearby medical offices became a cornerstone in American medicine –the Mayo Clinic. The brothers were physicians, scientists and humanitarians. They didn't hesitate in welcoming the unfortunate to their clinics and thirty percent of their patients were pleasantly surprised to receive their bills marked "Paid in Full." No one was charged more than ten percent of their annual income and every dollar collected on bills over $1,000 went to help other sick people. As successful as they became as physicians, they were even more successful as brothers and as humanitarians.

FLORENCE NIGHTINGALE (1820–1910)

Born in Florence, Italy of wealthy parents, she easily could have slipped into a life of luxury and pleasure. However, she possessed a strong spirit that inspired her to seek independence and a spiritual conscience that moved her toward a profession and service to God. In 1844, Florence decided to work in hospitals and, against her parents demands that "ladies" did not become nurses, she found some private nursing and a few months in a German school and hospital. She volunteered for service in the Crimean War in Turkey and struggled with the barbaric conditions of a field hospital. She created order and cleanliness, and mostly through the improvement of sanitary conditions, decreased the death rate by two-thirds. She led the reform of military hospitals and medical care and founded a school for the training of nurses. Her "Notes on Hospitals," published in 1859, gave detailed directions for the design of civilian hospitals.

LOUIS PASTEUR (1822–1895)

Born in the small town of Dole, France, the son of a tanner, Louis graduated from college at age eighteen with a degree in the arts. His doctorate was focused on the obscure science of crystallography which would have a decisive influence on his career. He was famous at age twenty-six when he demonstrated the phenomenon of optical isomers. In 1854, he became Professor of Chemistry and Dean of Sciences at the University of Lille and began his work on fermentation. He quickly designed experiments that eliminated the process of fermentation, thus developing the techniques of "pasteurization." This was not only helpful in the preserving of wine, beer, and milk, but also led to the reduction of infection in hospital operating rooms. Other scientific triumphs for the world of health included his work on germ theory and the development of vaccines. Sterilization of surgical instruments, steaming of bandages, controlling anthrax and a vaccine for rabies are just some of the results of his work.

JONAS EDWARD SALK (1914–1995)

Born in New York City, he entered the College of the City of New York at age sixteen to study law. He changed to medicine and graduated from the College of Medicine of New York University in 1939. In 1942, he went to the University of Michigan, where he developed an influenza vaccine. From there he moved to the University of Pittsburgh as associate professor of bacteriology and continued his research on a polio vaccine. By 1950, he had developed a vaccine against all three types of polio, and in 1955, after five years of testing, it was determined safe for the public. By the time he died, polio had disappeared from the United States. In 1963, he opened the Salk Institute for Biological Studies in San Diego, where he studied problems related to the body's rejection of organ transplants.

PUT HEALTH INTO ACTION

- Try to avoid "junk" food; snack on fruit and vegetables instead.
- Get some exercise every day.
- Get enough sleep to have energy throughout the day.
- Notice something beautiful in nature every day.
- Change a negative thought into a positive thought.
- Be aware of how great it is to feel healthy and strive to stay healthy.
- Play outside for awhile after school today.
- Choose healthy snacks instead of healthy ones for your school lunch.
- Create a chart showing the five food groups (be sure to show examples of each). Keep the chart where you can refer to it as the need arises.
- Develop good dental hygiene habits—brush, brush, brush!
- Wash your hands often with soap.
- Cover your mouth with a tissue when you sneeze.

COMMUNITY SERVICE IDEAS

- Volunteer with the Poison Control Center Booth in your town.
- Help stencil storm drains with warnings about toxic materials.
- Volunteer at a Health Fair; help organize one. (Arthritis Foundation)
- Volunteer at a park for some weeding and cleaning.
- Assist with fundraising and special events at the American Cancer Society.
- Make a mini-chart of the five food groups to take home and hang-up in your kitchen at home. It will remind you and your family to eat healthy everyday!
- Collect healthy recipes from family and friends. Then, as a class, combine these recipes into a healthy cookbook. Make copies for each student to take home.
- Take a mini-field-trip to explore the resources available at your school's clinic. Ask the school nurse for a tour.

BOOKS ON HEALTH

Gilgamesh, the King. Ludmila Zeman. Plattsburgh: Tundra Books, 1992

Green Man. Gail Haley. New York: Scribner, 1979.

A 3rd Serving of Chicken Soup for the Soul. Jack Canfield and Mark Victor Hansen. Deerfield Beach: Health Communications, Inc., 1996.

"The Beauty Remains; The Pain Passes" – p. 275

"A Lesson in Heart" – p. 262

A 4th Course of Chicken Soup for the Soul. Jack Canfield and Mark Victor Hansen. Deerfield Beach: Health Communications, Inc., 1997.

"State of Mind" – p. 326

A 5th Portion of Chicken Soup for the Soul. Jack Canfield and Mark Victor Hansen. Deerfield Beach: Health Communications, Inc., 1996.

"Consider This" – p. 301

"Puppy Love" – p. 336

"Soccer Balls and Violins" – p. 329

The Moral Compass. William J. Bennett, ed. New York: Simon and Schuster, 1995.

"The Prayer" – p. 751

May

SUPPORTIVE VALUES **Joy • Enthusiasm**

DEFINITIONS **The ability to see, express or enjoy the ridiculous, unexpected or unusual.**

When speaking of character traits or values we admire in a person, a sense of humor is often near the top of the list. Simply defined, **humor** is to discover, express, or appreciate the ludicrous, unexpected, or the absurd. Basically what we are referring to in regard to humor is anything which amuses us or makes us laugh and takes the edge off the seriousness in our sometimes too serious lives. The two kinds of humor which we want to focus on this month are best described by the following quotes: "A little nonsense now and then is relished by the wisest men," and "Happy is the person who can laugh at himself. He will never cease to be amused." We will focus on humor that allows us to enjoy the nonsense in life and encourage the ability to laugh at ourselves.

Our partner values of **joy** and **enthusiasm** refer to the attitudes which we have toward the way we live our lives. Joy is defined as a state of happiness or delight and enthusiasm is a feeling of strong excitement.

PURPOSE We are seeking to highlight humor, which enriches us by bringing joy and thus enthusiasm to our everyday lives. From a joyful and enthusiastic perspective we tend to treat others in a positive way, kindly and respectfully. We are all aware of humor which is unkind and disrespectful. It is, therefore, important that we recall our values of respect, kindness, and sincerity in our use of humor as teachers and also in the kind of humor we allow our students to use. Usually joy and enthusiasm are natural attributes of children, but the frequent, pseudo-sophisticated use of the word "boring" by many of our students speaks of neither joy nor enthusiasm. Joy can be found in the simplest of things, and an understanding of this hopefully can breed an enthusiasm for life and all it has to offer. This month we want to help instill an understanding of kind and respectful humor and the importance of joy and enthusiasm in our lives.

umor — May

Day One: Discuss the value of humor and what it means using the definitions on page 153. Learn about the origin of April Fools Day as a way to embrace the true spirit of humor.	**Day Two:** Go to the library and find a joke book. Memorize or copy one joke to share with your family at dinner tonight.	**Day Three:** Write or tell about telling your joke last night. Was it fun?	**Day Four:** Pair up with a classmate and teach each other your jokes. Try the new joke you learned on your family tonight!	**Day Five:** Create a Joker of the Week award to present to a classmate who has embraced humor all week. Do this every Friday for the rest of the month.
Day Six: Why is humor an important value? What would it be like if no one ever laughed? Share your thoughts in a small group.	**Day Seven:** Remember a time when you were laughed at or laughed at someone in a mean spirited manner. Draw a picture of your experience and think about why this was not the way to embrace the true meaning of humor.	**Day Eight:** Use the discussion questions on page 155 to learn more about the value of humor.	**Day Nine:** Draw a picture of yourself laughing. Hang all of these self-portraits up together for a truly gleeful collage!	**Day Ten:** Make a list of songs you know which are joyful. If you have any of these song at home—bring them in to share on Monday.
Day Eleven: As a class, choose some of the songs brought in to listen to. Let the music guide you to express your joy. Dance, close your eyes, draw to the music or do whatever the music moves you to do. After listening to the songs, discuss why these songs evoked joy.	**Day Twelve:** Select a bookmark from page 164 to decorate, cut out and use.	**Day Thirteen:** Read a story about humor from the collection on pages 157-163.	**Day Fourteen:** Choose and plan a community service project to encourage others to embrace humor. (see page 168 for ideas)	**Day Fifteen:** Engage in your community service plan.
Day Sixteen: Read about the heroes whose life stories are portrayed on pages 165-166. Which hero would you most like to emulate in your own life. Why?	**Day Seventeen:** Use the old saying "laugh and the world laughs with you, cry and you cry alone" as the theme of a creative story.	**Day Eighteen:** Smiling is the most simple and beautiful form of joy. Try to direct a smile to each of your classmates at least one time today.	**Day Nineteen:** Make a list of funny movies. Recommend ones you have seen or read reviews of to your classmates. Select one that you would like to watch with your family sometime soon. Tell why you selected that particular film.	**Day Twenty:** Reflect on what you have learned this month about humor. Make a practice of embracing humor in your life even when things seem tough!

HUMOR IN OTHER LANGUAGES

Chinese	————	There is no Chinese character for the meaning of humor. There is no concept of humor in the Asian mind.
French	*l'humour*	wit which focuses with drollness or fun upon the ridiculous, absurd, and unusual aspects of reality
German	*humor*	humor
Hawaiian	*ho'o makeaka*	"to cause laughter" (makeaka means "witty, comic, funny, amusing" and ho'o is a causative)
Japanese	*yuumoa*	a way of saying "humor" in Japanese (see Chinese)
Korean	*ik sal*	wisecrack, wit
Latin	*facetiae*	from Latin "umor" (body fluid) (Originally our word "humor" came from the Latin word "umor" meaning a body fluid. It took on the meaning of "disposition." If your "humors" were bad, you were in a poor disposition . . . bad mood. Your "humors" determined your nature.)
Spanish	*humor*	humor, wit, mood
Tagalog	*katatawanan*	a funny quality; a joke or jest; seeing the funny side of life

DISCUSSION QUESTIONS

- Why is it so much fun to laugh?
- Why does it make you feel good?
- Do you think laughing is healthy? Why?
- What is the difference between having fun and making fun of someone? Why isn't it funny to that person?
- What are the things that make you really happy? Why?
- What can you do to make others happy?
- What does it mean to have a sense of humor?
- Why is it healthy to laugh at oneself?
- What is the difference between laughing at someone and laughing with someone?
- How would you describe the phrase "filled with joy?" What would take away this feeling?
- What things have to be present in your life for you to be happy? Are they things or people?

STORIES AND THOUGHTS FROM SPIRITUAL TRADITIONS

Hinduism

Where there is joy, there is creation. Where there is no joy, there is no creation.

– Upanishads

Buddhism

Be friendly to all and speak with gentle words. It is easy to love those who are lovable, but difficult to love those who are nasty and gruff. So whether people are rich or poor, educated or uneducated, acquaintances or strangers, the challenge is to be equally friendly and kind to all.

Christianity

"A cheerful heart is good medicine." *– Proverbs 17:22*

"To make an apt answer is a joy and a word in season, how good it is!"
– Proverbs 15:25

David Dances Before the Ark

David brought the Ark to the city of David with a great celebration. After the men who were carrying it had gone, David danced before the Lord with all his might. So Israel brought home the Ark of the Lord with great joy.

But as the procession came into the city, Michal, Saul's daughter, watched from a window and saw King David leaping and dancing before the Lord; and she was filled with contempt for him.

The Ark was placed inside the tent which David had prepared for it; and he sacrificed burnt offerings and peace offerings to the Lord. Then he blessed the people in the name of the Lord, and gave a present to everyone—men and women alike. When it was all over, and everyone had gone home, David returned to bless his family.

But Michal came out to meet him and exclaimed in disgust, "How glorious the king of Israel looked today! He exposed himself to the girls along the street like a common pervert!"

David retorted, "I was dancing before the Lord who chose me above your father and his family and who appointed me as a leader of Israel, the people of the Lord! So I am willing to act like a fool in order to show my joy in the Lord. Yes, and I am willing to look more foolish than this . . . "

– Bible, II Samuel 6:12-21

India

The Hunter of Justice

Pramod of our village was working in the city. I must admit that nobody else from our village was employed in the city, and only a few had occasionally visited it.

Pramod walked and talked in a very superior way. He look down on everybody in the village. He spoke of the city as if it was a fairyland!

No doubt, he commanded some respect from the people of his own age. So far as the elders were concerned, they just tolerated him.

But how would the children of the village understand that he had any reason to be proud? Why should Mintu, Rintu, Raghu and Bapi show him any respect?

One day while the children were playing in the village square, Pramod happened to pass by. Now, the children played a game called 'Strike the Stick'. They would set a stick on the sands. Then, from a certain distance, they would throw another stick at it. One who could strike the target at the first throw would gain a point.

It was Mintu's turn to hurl the stick. He hurled it; but suddenly Pramod came between him and the target. Mintu's stick hit Pramod's leg.

"You loafer! I will teach you how to behave!" yelled Pramod. He rushed at Mintu, but Mintu ran away. Pramod tried to catch him, but in vain. Can a bull ever catch a mongoose?

The angry Pramod reported the matter to Mintu's father Ranganath.

I'm sorry, Pramod, I will ask the boy and his friends, not to change the village square into a playground!" said Ranganath.

"That is all right," said Pramod with some disgust, "but what about the mischief your son has already done?"

"It is not his mischief, Pramod, it is his mistake. Don't you remember how you and I too used to play the same game?" Ranganath reminded him smiling politely.

But it had no effect on Pramod. "I want justice!" he shouted.

"I see," said Ranganath gravely. "In that case you have to complain to Chowdhury!"

Chowdhury was a highly revered figure in that area. His was the last word on any dispute. People accepted his judgements without any murmur.

Chowdhury lived in an adjoining village. As Pramod headed in that direction, he came face to face with Diwakar.

"Hello, Pramod, why must you walk so fast? What is the matter with you?" asked Diwaker. Pramod gave the reason. But Diwakar smiled and said, "Pramod, must you grow so very angry for such a trifle? Have peace!"

"It is easy to lecture on peace!" shouted Pramod. "I want justice!"

"Very well. Go ahead!" said Diwakar.

Chowdhury was amused at Pramod's complaint, but he did not show that he had taken the complaint lightly. Instead, he said, "You see, such cases are judged by Diwakar of you village. I give my attention to other kinds of cases!"

"But Diwakar only knows how to lecture on peace. He does not understand the need for justice!" complained Pramod.

"You tell him that I want him to do justice in this case," said Chowdhury. But Pramod was not satisfied. He brought Diwakar to Chwodhury. Diwakar promised to do justice.

Back in their village, Diwakar called all the respectable men of the village and placed Pramod's case before them: "Mintu is to blame for his conduct. Pramod should either forgive him or punish him. Pramod is bent on punishing him. What do you say?" he asked.

Mishra, the headmaster of the village school, said, "Mintu has not struck Pramod deliberately. That is why it will not be proper for Pramod to strike Mintu deliberately. He can only throw a stick at Mintu's leg."

"That is correct," agreed all.

"But Mintu may run away. How can I throw a stick at him?" asked Pramod.

"Mintu shall be held by two of us. But see to it that your stick strikes only Mintu, not the others!" cautioned Diwakar.

But it was not necessary to hold Mintu. He stood on his own. Pramod took aim and hurled a stick at his legs, but it missed them. He was given two more chances, but he missed them. Those present could not check their laughter. Pramod felt terribly humiliated. He fled.

"Mintu, If you kept standing today without any fear, what made you run away when Pramod wanted to catch you?" Diwakar asked the boy, giving him a pat on the back.

"I did not know how he would have punished me then. Now, before all my guardians, he could not have done anything he liked. What is more, my father assured me that Uncle Pramod was his playmate and that Uncle Pramod could never hit his target!"

There was an uproarious laughter. Pramod left for the city the same day.

Japanese

The Terrible Eek

One very stormy night, there was a family tucked into their little thatched house in the mountains. The father and son sat warming their hands over a small fire while the mother went about preparing their supper. The rain fell heavily on the little house and the strong winds shook its walls. The noises of the storm began to frighten the little boy and meekly he looked up at his father and asked "Papa, are you ever afraid?"

"Oh yes, son, there are things which frighten me," nodded his father.

"What is it that frightens you most in the world?" asked the boy.

"Well, among humans, it is a thief that frightens me most," answered the father.

Now it just so happened that a thief was climbing on the roof of that very house, hoping to steal something on that dark and rainy night. When he heard the father's answer to his son's question he was filled with pride. "I am what they fear most in the world! How strong and powerful I am!"

The father continued to answer his son. "Among animals, I must say that I fear the wolf the most."

At that very moment there was a wolf creeping just under the window of the little house, hoping to steal a chicken for his dinner. Upon hearing the father's words he laughed proudly.

"I am what they fear most in the world! How strong and powerful I am!"

"But the most frightening thing of all," the father continued,"especially on a night like tonight, is a terrible leak. I truly hope there are no leaks tonight!"

The sounds of the wind and rain had grown quite loud, and the wolf strained to hear the father's words. "Did he say a terrible eek? Why, I've never heard of an eek before, but if it is what frightens him most of all it must be very fearsome indeed!" thought the wolf.

The thief high on the roof could barely hear the father's words between the gusts of wind. "Did he say he was afraid of a terrible eek?" wondered the thief. "I don't know what an eek is, but if it is what he fears most in the world it must be horrible!"

Just then, a great gust of wind knocked the thief over and he slid uncontrollably down the wet roof and landed with a thump right on the back of the wolf. The thief was so surprised to feel something wet and furry beneath him that he was certain that he had landed on an eek. And the wolf, surprised by the sudden burden on his back, thought surely it must be an eek gripping him tightly around the neck. With a great howl, the wolf began running with all his might through the trees while the thief clung with all his might to the wolf's back. The terrified wolf tore through the forest thinking, "Oh no! How will I ever get this eek off my back?" And the terrified thief thought as they sped along, "Oh no! How will I ever get off the back of this eek?"

Then all at once, the thief spied a low-hanging branch. He reached up and caught it as the wolf shot out from under him. But the branch was too weak to hold the thief, and it snapped and he fell. Now it just so happened that there was a deep hole right next to the tree and the thief fell into it. He tried to climb out, but it was too deep and the sides too slippery.

Meanwhile, the wolf, quite relieved to have the burden off his back ran back to his den. Quite breathless, he stopped at a stream to drink and there, he met a tiger. "What's the matter, Wolf?" inquired the tiger. You look as though you've had quite a fright."

"Oh yes, I have. I've just had the most terrible eek jump on my back. It gripped me by the neck and I ran and ran until finally, it let go."

"Why, I've never heard of a terrible eek in my life." laughed the tiger.

"Humans fear it more than anything," said the wolf, "and now I understand why. It is a terrible and fearsome thing."

"But I am the most powerful and fearsome creature that humans are afraid of!" cried the tiger. "I will find this terrible eek and catch him just to prove it!"

So the wolf and tiger set off into the forest. They had not gone far when they met a monkey. "What are you two doing at this time of night?" the monkey inquired.

"We're off to catch the terrible eek," replied the tiger.

"I've never heard of a terrible eek," said the monkey.

"It's the most fearsome creature in the world," said the wolf. "I know because there was one on my back not too long ago."

"I would like to see you catch this creature. I'm coming along," said monkey.

The wolf led the monkey and the tiger back to the tree where the thief had jumped off. They spotted the deep hole and wolf whispered, "I think it might be down there."

"Are you in there, terrible eek?" roared the tiger. But there was no response. The thief was certain that the eek had come back to get him, and so he remained silent.

Winking at the others, the monkey said, "I will lower my tail into the hole. The eek will grab onto it. You catch him as soon as he's out of the hole." The others nodded.

Slowly, the monkey lowered his furry tail into the hole. The thief grabbed onto the tail and pulled hard. The monkey became frightened and pulled back even harder, trying to recover his tail. But the thief held fast. The wolf pulled on the monkey, and the tiger pulled on the wolf with such force that the thief came flying out of the hole, letting out an enormous cry. The cry startled the monkey, who screamed, "It's an eek!"

"Oh no, it's an eek!" cried the wolf, turning to the tiger.

"Oh no, an EEEEEEEEEEEEEK!" screeched the tiger.

"EEEEEEEEEEEEEEK!" hollered the thief.

All the noise and ruckus scared each one so much that they all ran off in different directions, each hoping that the eek was not following them.

Meanwhile, all snug in their little thatched house was the family preparing for bed.

"Goodnight, son," said the father.

"Goodnight, papa. It's a good thing there were no terrible leaks tonight," said the son.

"You're right, son," said the father. "There were no terrible leaks."

PROVERBS AND MAXIMS

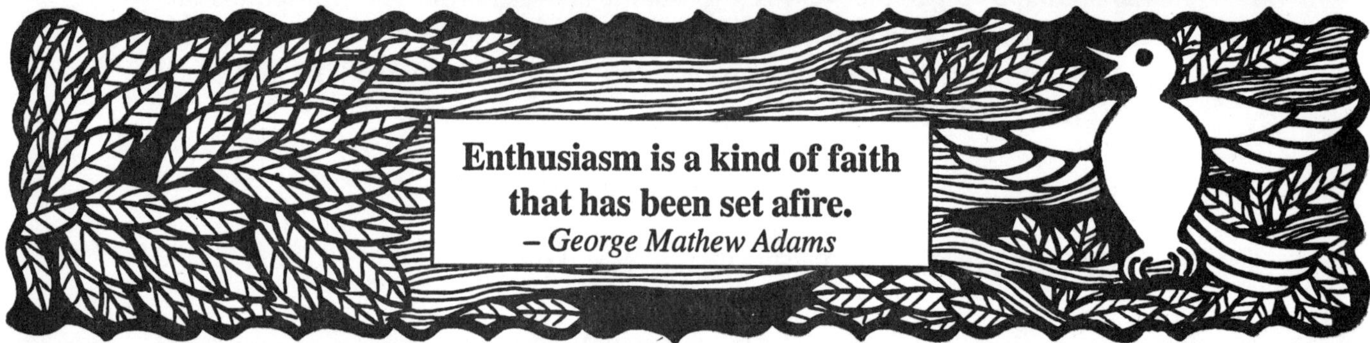

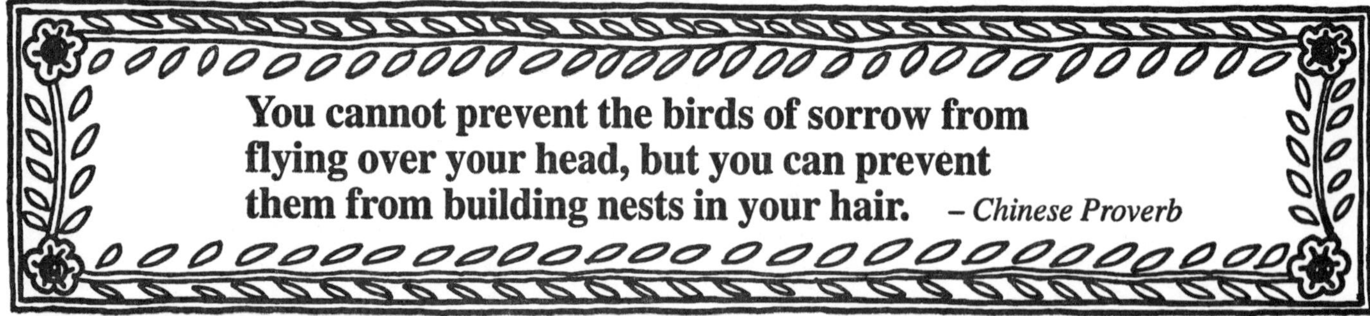

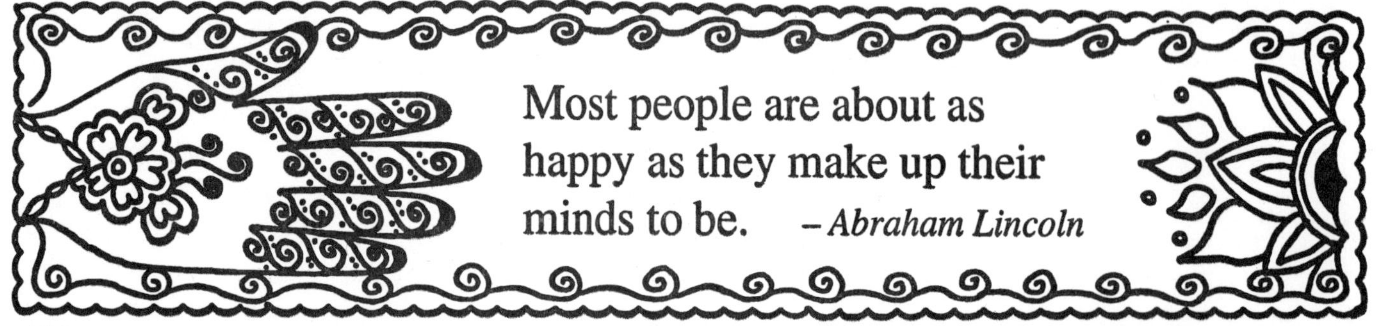

HEROES AND HEROINES

LUCILLE BALL (1911–1989)

Born in Celeron, New York, a suburb of Jamestown near Lake Chautauqua, Lucille derived from her grandfather, a woodturner in a furniture factory, her instinct for family loyalty and for survival by hard work. As a child, she loved going to vaudeville shows and movies and then acting out what she had seen. She failed at a New York City dramatic school and was either fired from or not called for several shows. She worked as a soda jerk and a model before she became known as the Chesterfield Cigarette Girl, and had a chance for a movie role in 1933. Over the next few years and many bit parts in films, she recognized her strength in comedy and gradually increased her $50 a week salary to $3,500 a week. Her "universal language of wacky humor" and her irrepressible optimism finally paid off when the "I Love Lucy Show" premiered in 1951. It became one of TV's four all-time hits, and she was awarded the title "Comedienne of the Century" in 1964.

ERMA LOUISE FISTE BOMBECK (1927–1996)

Born in Dayton, Ohio, she has been described as a housewife turned humorist. She had the uncanny ability to take everyday occurrences and annoyances and, writing with wry humor, turn them into delightful anecdotes that helped Americans laugh at themselves. She graduated with a degree in English from the University of Dayton and began her writing career with the Journal Herald in Dayton, where she wrote obituaries and stories for the women's page. She married William Lawrence Bombeck in 1949 and put her writing aside when they adopted their first child in 1953. In 1964, she began writing a humor column, which was syndicated within weeks; at the peak of the column's success, her humor was enjoyed by a readership of 30 million people in over 900 newspapers. She wrote eleven books and made regular appearances on the "Good Morning America" show. She and her husband were generous members of their community and contributed many hours of volunteer work, especially with the American Red Cross.

BILL COSBY (1937–)

Born in the Germantown district of North Philadelphia, Pennsylvania as William Henry Cosby, Jr., Bill grew up in an all-black housing project. His father was a Navy mess steward and his mother worked as a domestic. His father was away a lot but his mother read to him regularly from the Bible and Mark Twain, teaching him to stay away from the dangers of the inner city ghetto. As a child, he was inspired by the comedian Sid Caesar and he earned the reputation of "an alert boy who would rather clown than study" (so writes a sixth-grade teacher). Bill dropped out of school in the tenth grade and joined the navy, where he earned a high school equivalency diploma. He went to college on a track and field scholarship at Temple University in Philadelphia, earning a degree in Physical Education. His career in comedy began in college when he took a part-time job tending bar and telling jokes in a Philadelphia coffeehouse, the Cellar. Today, Bill has a successful career as the dominant comedic voice of black Americans.

WILL ROGERS (1879–1935)

Born in his parents' ranch house between the Oklahoma towns of Claremore and Oologah, he was named William Penn Adair Rogers. His father, Clem, and mother, Mary, were part Cherokee and that part of Oklahoma was still Indian territory when he was born. Will was a very bright young boy and was offered an excellent education, but he wasn't interested in school and chose to speak with a Western drawl. He inherited his mother's easygoing manner and sense of humor. He became one of America's most loved characters and achieved great success as a philosopher, columnist, movie star, radio personality, and philanthropist. His humor poked fun at hypocrisy, smugness, and greed, even at the very famous. He did this with such genuine humor that everyone loved him. He loved to travel and wasn't afraid to take risks. His love of flying, when it was still dangerous, led to his early death. While on a flight around the world, he crashed with his good friend Wiley Post in Point Darrow, Alaska.

RED SKELTON (1913–1997)

Born in Vincennes, Indiana as Richard Bernard Skelton, he was the only redhead in the family and soon acquired the nickname that he was to adopt as his first name. He began his professional career at age ten, working as a medicine show singer, a tent-show performer, a circus clown, and a showboat comedian. He was the youngest of burlesque comedians at age sixteen. His formal schooling ended with the seventh grade when he left home to take up show business. He married Edna Stillwell when he was eighteen in 1931, struggled through the depression, and finally experienced some success in 1936. He was soon appearing regularly on the radio and making movies. He continued performing in clubs and comedy concerts through the 1980s. He also wrote music and did paintings of clown faces. He possessed broad antic talents of pantomime, mugging, and knockabout routines. He is well known for his characterizations of the Mean Widdle Kid, the mute hobo Freddie the Freeloader, and the simple-minded rustic Clem Kadiddlehopper.

MARK TWAIN (1835–1910)

Born in Florida, Missouri as Samuel Langhorne Clemens, he was the son of a storekeeper who was also at times a lawyer who struggled with success. Failure in business moved the Clemens family to Hannibal, Missouri, which became the hometown of Sam Clemens and the town that played significant roles in some of his finest work. His experiences in Hannibal as a boy, his work as a steamboat pilot and reporter on the western frontier, and his travels abroad provided him with the experiences and materials for most of his successful writing. He had very little formal education and his work varied in excellence because of his natural tendency to write intuitively and with improvisation. His successful novels charmed the American public because of their humor and their portrayal of the life and times of 19th Century America; *The Adventures of Tom Sawyer* (1876) and *The Adventures of Huckleberry Finn* (1884) will remain as American classics. His travels, his unique historical perspectives, and his tendency to speak his mind produced essays, articles, and humorous sketches about life in America. He launched another career as a humorous lecturer and enjoyed taking advantage of the foibles of politics and religion.

PUT HUMOR INTO ACTION

- Smile when you say "good morning."
- Laugh a little every day.
- Do something for someone that you know will make them happy.
- Be enthusiastic about something.
- Tell a joke.
- Listen to a joke.
- Read a funny story.
- Share a cartoon that you thought was funny.
- Laugh at yourself if you make a mistake or do something silly.
- Talk with people about the humor in life.
- Take moments to "lighten up"; be serious when necessary but don't take everything seriously, especially yourself.
- Share a funny experience that happened at school today with someone at home tonight.

COMMUNITY SERVICE IDEAS

- Rent a video of a comedy from the 40's and show it at a retirement home.
- Make placemats decorated with cartoons and jokes for hospital patients.
- Organize a group of friends (or your soccer team or scout troop) and put on a funny play for a children's hospital.
- Put on a puppet show for your classmates.
- Make a sign or banner reminding people to smile! (You may even include a joke on the sign.) Hang it up in a public place.
- Make a clown's face by decorating an oval-shaped cut-out piece of cardboard. Everyone should wear their mask for a set period of time to remind members of the group of the value of humor!

BOOKS ON HUMOR

The Lady Who Saw the Good Side of Everything. Pat Tapio. New York: Seabury Press, 1975.

A Light in the Attic. Shel Silverstein. New York: Harper & Row, 1981.

The Old Dog Barks Backwards. Ogden Nash. Boston: Little, Brown, 1972.

Where the Sidewalk Ends. Shel Silverstein. New York: Harper & Row, 1974.

The Book of Virtues. William J. Bennett, ed. New York: Simon and Schuster, 1993.
"The Bear and the Travelers" – p. 271

A Call to Character. Colin Greer and Herbert Kohl, eds. New York: Harper Collins Publishers, 1995.
"Alice in Wonderland" – p. 143
"Coyote, Coyote, Please Tell Me" – p. 355
"How the Hot Ashes Shovel Helped Snoo Foo" – p. 136
"The Laugher" – p. 133
"Mary Poppins" – p. 128
"Pippi Longstocking" – p. 119
"The Sword of Wood" – p. 126

RESOURCES FOR THE CLASSROOM

The Book of Virtues. William J. Bennett ed. New York: Simon and Schuster, 1993.

A Call to Character. Colin Greer and Herbert Kohl eds. New York: Harper Collins Publishers, 1995.

Chicken Soup for the Soul. Jack Canfield and Mark Victor Hansen. New York: Guideposts, 1993.

Chicken Soup for the Teenage Soul. Jack Canfield, "etal." Deerfield Beach: Health Communications, Inc., 1997.

A 2nd Helping of Chicken Soup for the Soul. Jack Canfield and Mark Victor Hansen. New York: Guideposts, 1995.

A 3rd Serving of Chicken Soup for the Soul. Jack Canfield and Mark Victor Hansen. New York: Guideposts, 1996.

A 4th Course of Chicken Soup for the Soul. Jack Canfield "etal." New York: Guideposts, 1997.

A 5th Portion of Chicken Soup for the Soul. Jack Canfield and Mark Victor Hansen. New York: Guideposts, 1996.

The Moral Compass. William J. Bennett ed. New York: Simon and Schuster, 1995.

Is Your Bed Still There When You Close the Door? Jane M. Healy. New York: Doubleday, 1992.

GENERAL RESOURCES

Books to Build On—A Grade-by-Grade Resource Guide for Parents and Teachers. John Holdren and E.D. Hirsch, Jr., eds. New York: Delta, 1996.

Educating for Character: How our schools can teach respect and responsibility. Thomas Lickona. New York: Bantam, 1991.

The Fifth Discipline. Peter M. Senge. New York: Doubleday, 1990.

Greater Expectations: Overcoming the culture of indulgence in America's homes and schools. William Damon. New York: Free Press, 1995.

How Good People Make Tough Choices. Rushworth M. Kidder. New York: Morrow, 1994.

Positive Discipline. Jane Nelson. New York: Ballantine Books, 1987.

Reclaiming Our Schools: A Handbook on Teaching Character, Academics, and Discipline. 2nd ed. Edward A. Wynne and Kevin Ryan. New Jersey: Prentice-Hall, 1996.

HEROES IN BOOKS

The Great Kapok Tree: A Tale of the Amazon Rainforest. Lynne Cherry. San Diego: Harcourt Brace, Jovanovich, 1990.

Beethoven Lives Upstairs. Barbara Nichol. New York: Orchard Books, 1994.

Lives of the Musicians. Kathleen Krull. San Diego: Harcourt Brace, Jovanovich, 1992.

Galileo. Leonard Everett Fisher. New York: Macmillan Publishing Company, 1992.

Shaka, King of the Zulu. Diane Stanley. New York: Marrow Junior Books, 1988.

The Great Alexander the Great. Joe Lasker. New York: Viking Press, 1983.

Theseus and the Minotaur. C. J. Naden. Mahwah: Troll Associates, 1981.

Perseus and Medusa. C. J. Naden. Mahwah: Troll Associates, 1981.

The Voyage of Osires: a myth of ancient Egypt. Gerold McDermott. New York: Windmill Books, 1977.

The Sword in the Stone. Hudson Talbott. New York: Books of Wonder, 1991.

Johnny Appleseed: a tall tale. Steven Kellogg. New York: Morrow Junior Books, 1988.

Wolferl: the first six years in the life of Wolfgang Amadeus Mozart. Lisl Weil. New York: Holiday House, 1991.

Paul Bunyan, A Tall Tale. Steven Kellogg. New York: W. Morrow, 1984.

Go Free or Die: a story about Harriet Tubman. Jerry Ferris. Minneapolis: Carolrhoda Books, 1988.

What's the Big Idea Ben Franklin?. Jean Fritz. New York: Coward, McCann, Geoghegan, 1976.

Honest Abe. Edith Kunhardt. New York: Greenwillow Books, 1993.

Gilgamesh the King. Ludmila Zeman. Montreal: Tundra Books, 1992.

The Trojan Horse. Warwick Hutton. New York: Margaret K. McElderry Books, 1992.

Mother Teresa, sister to the poor. Patricia Giff. New York: Viking Kestrel, 1986.

Good Queen Bess. Diane Stanley. New York: Four WInds Press, 1990.

Jane Goodall. Eleanor Coerr. New York: Putnam, 1976.

OTHER RESOURCES

Against Borders:
Promoting Books for a Multicultural World. Hazel Rochman. Chicago: American Library Association, 1993.

The Best Years of Their Lives:
A Resource Guide for Teenagers in Crisis. Stephanie Zvirin. Chicago: American Library Association, 1992.
A selective, annotative bibliography of fiction and non-fiction self-help works for teenagers, arranged under the following topics: Family matters, School daze, Me, myself, and I, Crack, glue, or a six-pack or two?, Private property: don't touch, Wellness, Sex stuff, One plus one makes three, and Death: romance and reality.

What Would We Do Without You?
A Guide to Volunteer Activities for Kids. Kathy Henderson. White Hall: Betterway Publications, 1990.

Brothers, A Hebrew Legend.
Florence Freedman. New York: Harper & Row, 1985.
This tale of brotherly love exemplifies the values of responsibility, compassion, generosity, commitment, sharing, and family.

Fables.
Tana Reiff. Syracuse: New Readers Press, 1991.

When I Grew Up Long Ago:
family living, going to school, games and parties, cure and death, a comet, falling in love, and other things I remember. Alvin Shwartz. Philadelphia: Lippincott, 1978.
Values from the "good old days."

The Newbery Award Reader:
A Collection of Short Fiction by Writers Who Have Won the John Newbery Medal. Charles G. Waugh and Martin H. Greenberg eds. San Diego: Harcourt Brace Jovanovich, 1984.

BIBLIOGRAPHY

Resources for Buddhism

Tokunaga, Keiko, Graduate Student in Zen Buddhism, University of Hawaii, Honolulu, Hawaii.
Tsomo, Karma Lekshe, Philosophy Department, University of Hawaii, Honolulu, Hawaii.

Resources for Chinese Religions

Hsuan, Ko, (Aleister Crowley). *Tao Te Ching*. Maine: Samuel Weiser, Inc., 1995.
Ware, James R. *The Sayings of Confucius*. New York: Mentor Books, 1955

Resources for Christianity

The Living Bible. Illinois: Tyndale House Publishers, 1971.

Resources for Hawaiian Stories

Alameida, Roy. *Stories of Old Hawaii*. Honolulu: Bess Press, 1997.
Kawaharada, Dennis. *Hawaiian Fishing Legends*. Honolulu: Kalamaka Press, 1992.
Pukui, Mary Kawena. *Folktales of Hawai'i*. Honolulu: Bishop Museum Press, 1995.
Pukui, Mary Kawena. *'Olelo No'eau*. Honolulu: Bishop Museum Press, 1983.
Pukui, Mary Kawena. *The Water of Kane*. Honolulu: Kamehameha Schools Press, 1951.
Thompson, Vivian L. *Hawaiian Myths of Earth Sea and Sky*. New York: Holiday, 1996.

Resources for Hinduism

Bhagavad Gita. Trans. Prabhavananda, Swami, and Christopher Isherwood. New York: Mentor Books, 1944.
The Upanishads. Trans. Prabhavananda, Swami, and Frederick Manchester. New York: Mentor Books, 1948.

Resources for Stories from India

Ayier, V.A.K., *Stories of Vikramaditya*. Bombay: Dharatyia Vidya Bhavan, 1974.
Chandamama, Chandamama Publications: Vadapalani, Madras, India, December 1989, March 1994, April 1994.
Lao, Chaman. *Spiritual Stories of India*. Delhi: Publications Division, Ministry of Information & Broadcasting, Government of India
Vivekananda, Swami. *Stories for Children*. Calcutta: Advaita Ashrama, 1994.

Resources for Islam

Rumi, Jalal ad-Din. *Discourses of Rumi*. Trans. A.J. Arberry. Great Britain: Curzon Press, 1993
Brown, Kerry and Martin Palmer. *The Essential Teachings of Islam*. London: Century Hutchinson Ltd., ed. 1987

Darbanid, Afkham and Dick Davis, translators of Farid ud-Din Attar's work, *The Conference of the Birds*. New York: Penguin Books Ltd., 1984.
Fazl, Mirza Abu'l, ed. and translator, Selections from Mishkat-ul-Masabih, *Chowk Minar Anarkali Lahore*. Pakistan: Sind Sagar Academy, 1977.
The Effendi and the Pregnant Pot. Trans. Primerose Gigliesi and Robert C. Friend. Beijing: New World Press, 1982.
Khan, Maulana Wahiduddin. *God-oriented Life: In the Light of Sayings and Deeds of the Prophet Muhammad and his Companions.* New Delhi: Islamic Centre, 1992.
Nizam ad-Din Awliya: Morals for the Heart. Trans. Bruce B. Lawrence. New York: Paulist Press, 1992.
Rumi, Jalal ad-Din. Trans. Reynold A. Nicholson. *Rumi: Poet and Mystic.* London: George Allen and Unwin Ltd.,1968.
Rumi, Jalal ad-Din. Trans. E.H. Whinfield. *Teachings of Rumi: The Masnavi of Maulana Jalalu-'d-Din Muhammad I Rumi.* New York: E.P. Dutton & Co., Inc., 1975.
Yusaf, Ali Abdullah. *The Meaning of the Holy Qur'an.* Brentwood, Maryland: Amana Corporation, 1992.

Resources for Judaism

Buber, Martin. *Tales of the Hasidi.* New York: Schocken Books, 1975.
Fahs, Sophia Lyon and Alice Cobb. *Old Tales for a New Day.* New York: Prometheus Books, 1992.
Schwartz, Howard. *Gabriel's Palace, retold.* Oxford: Oxford University Press, 1993.

Resources for Stories from Other Cultures

Compton, Patricia A. *The Terrible Eek.* New York: Simon and Schuster, 1991.
Demi. *The Empty Pot.* New York: H. Holt, 1990
Freedman, Florence. *Brothers: A Hebrew Legend.* New York: Harper and Row, 1985.
Gerson, Mary-Joan. *Why the Sky is Far Away.* New York: Harcourt Brace, Jovanovich, 1974.
Goble, Paul. *Love Flute.* New York: Maxwell MacMillan International, 1992.
Han, Carolyn. *Tales from Within the Cloud.* Honolulu: University of Hawaii Press, 1997.
Heady, Eleanor B. *Jambo, Sungura.* New York: W.W. Norton and Co., 1965.
Kendall, Carol and Yao-wen Li. *Sweet and Sour Tales from China.* New York: The Seabury Press, 1979.
McDermott, Gerald. *The Stonecutter.* New York: Viking Press, 1975.
Polacco, Patricia. *Appelamando's Dreams.* New York: Philomel Books, 1991.
Rosen, Michael. *Crow and Hawk.* San Diego: Harcourt Brace, 1995.
San Souci, Robert D. *The Faithful Friend.* New York: Simon and Schuster, 1995.
Sierra, Judy. *Wiley and the Hairy Man.* New York: Dutton Children's Books, 1996.
Uchida, Yoshiko. *The Wise Old Woman.* New York: Maxwell MacMillan International, 1994.
Waite, Michael P. *Jojofu.* New York: Lothrop, Lee and Shepard Books, 1996.